Ink Trails

Marquette
Carroll Watson Rankin

Ishpeming
John Donaldson Voelker

Elk Rapids
Eugene Ruggles

Benzonia
Charles Bruce Catton
Sara Gwendolyn Frostic

Saginaw
Theodore Huebner Roethke

Owosso
James Oliver Curwood

Lapeer
Marguerite de Angeli

Robert Frost
Jane Kenyon
Arthur Miller

Henrietta Township
Holling Clancy Holling

Ann Arbor

South Haven
Liberty Hyde Bailey

Grass Lake
Maritta Wolff

Detroit
Dudley Felker Randall

Saline
George Matthew Adams

Tower Hill & Harbert
Carl Sandburg

Niles
Ringgold Wilmer Lardner

Hudson
William McKendree Carleton

Ink Trails

Michigan's Famous and Forgotten Authors

DAVE DEMPSEY *and* JACK DEMPSEY

Michigan State University Press

East Lansing

♾ The paper used in this publication meets the minimum requirements of
ANSI/NISO Z39.48-1992 (R 1997) (Permanence of Paper).

Michigan State University Press
East Lansing, Michigan 48823-5245

Printed and bound in the United States of America.

18   17   16   15   14   13   12   1   2   3   4   5   6   7   8   9   10

LIBRARY OF CONGRESS CATALOGING-IN-PUBLICATION DATA
Dempsey, Dave, 1957–
    Ink trails : Michigan's famous and forgotten authors / Dave Dempsey and Jack Dempsey.
    p.   cm.
    Includes bibliographical references.
    ISBN 978-1-61186-060-3 (pbk. : alk. paper) 1. Authors, American—
Homes and haunts—Michigan. 2. American literature—Michigan. 3. Michigan—
Intellectual life. 4. Michigan—In literature. I. Dempsey, Jack, 1952– II. Title.
    PS283.M5D46   2012
    810.9'32774—dc23
    2011050533

Frontispiece map by E. White
Book and cover design by Erin Kirk New
Original cover art by Erin Kirk New includes a map by Ellen White and
    work from ©iStockphoto.com / Cheryl Graham.

g green press Michigan State University Press is a member of the Green Press Initiative
and is committed to developing and encouraging ecologically responsible publishing
practices. For more information about the Green Press Initiative and the use of recycled
paper in book publishing, please visit www.greenpressinitiative.org.

Visit Michigan State University Press at www.msupress.org

To Jennifer and Suzzanne

Contents

Acknowledgments

Many thanks to the following people for their generous assistance in securing photos, and for helping us understand part of the story of the authors we discuss:

Marguerite de Angeli—Kate A. Pohjola, director of the Lapeer District Library, who patiently provided biographical information and photographs of her hometown author.

Bruce Catton—Bill and Carol Bedford, Crystal Lake denizens, whose photo research and encouragement were invaluable.

Holling Clancy Holling—Joan Hoffman, whose stewardship of the Holling life story and works is inspirational.

Theodore Roethke—Michelle Hurd Riddick and David Riddick of Saginaw. They know why we appreciate them.

Eugene Ruggles—niece Lisa Wyatt Knowlton and longtime friend Delia Moon, who called our attention to this Michigan-born poet and provided photographs from their family and personal files.

John Voelker—Fred Baker and the Voelker family, for gracious permission to use special photos, and for flyspecking the manuscript.

Maritta Wolff—Laura and Hugh Stegman, Maritta Wolff's daughter-in-law and son, respectively. They spent considerable time telling us the story of the remarkable Maritta Wolff, and rummaged through their papers to find photographs.

And our thanks to Jacqueline Tinney for able assistance with the manuscript.

Introduction

Dave Dempsey

As far back as I can remember, books owned me. By the time I was five, I was regularly accompanying my family to a Dearborn library, checking out the maximum number of books—which I remember as four. I returned them and took the quota again as quickly as I could. Occasionally my parents indulged me by paying for my selections from the Scholastic Book Service catalog. That was a significant gift in a family of five making it on a professor's income in the mid-1960s.

I began with books like *Mike Mulligan and His Steam Shovel*, whose illustrations I can see vividly a half century later. (Steam shovel Mary Anne's eyes and smile as she settled into a lifetime in the basement with Mike are especially clear.) Later, the stories within the covers of the Landmark Series, children's-level biographies, and the "vulgar" *Hardy Boys* series that no library seemed to hold were an incubator for my imagination, but also a refuge from what I sometimes regarded as a hostile society. As I read books, I wanted to create them, and I wondered how it was done. I wondered who the people were who could call themselves "authors."

Like the tales that played out on my imagination's stage, the mental pictures I created of these writers tantalized me. I pictured night owls plunking out words on old typewriters during sleepless nights. I saw poets lying on their backs in the grass on summer days, dreaming up poems about the transience of beauty.

I'm not conscious of thinking specifically about any authors related to Michigan—until I picked up a series of books on the Civil War that my father and older brother, the coauthor of this book, had already read. Bruce Catton wrote with grace and dramatic flair. Who was this man and what had made him such a good writer? I got a hint of the answer simply by riding through, and later driving through, and sometimes even stopping in, the small town of Benzonia. Catton and his hometown is for me the genesis of this book.

Ernest Hemingway was a later, acquired taste. He was more difficult to love, but no more difficult to admire. Probably every reader of his who dares to write imitates his prose style for months or years afterward (I was no exception, but I couldn't pull it off). Northern Michigan touched Hemingway and touched Catton, but with remarkably different results. Perhaps that's in part because a small, secure village helped school Catton in a benign world of fixed truths, while a moody lake and second-growth woods extracted the wildness within Hemingway. Michigan contains those contrasts. But a multitude of other explanations make equal or greater sense.

Reading the chapters Jack and I have created, I see several running themes. As an environmental advocate (who now prefers to call himself a conservationist), I am most struck by the thought that Michigan's forests, dunes, farmland, and water were the cradle of creativity for almost all of the authors profiled. For those most influenced by their Michigan towns or cities, I like to think something in their communities, as small as the village green or vast as the sky, helped foster their art.

In the end, of course, the truth is place. Place is where we first become conscious of a world outside ourselves, then outside the family, then outside the community. Place is where we draw our first and last breath. Place either smothers our spirit or liberates it. A startlingly beautiful and varied place like Michigan most often frees the spirit. In doing so, it is parent to creativity—sometimes everlasting art.

I thank my older brother and dedicated historian Jack for conceiving and helping shoulder the burden of work for this book. It would never have happened without him. I thank my younger brother Tom for his fascination with words and his love of travel—the fruition of his imagination. And I thank my parents for showing me the world of books and their authors at an early age.

Introduction

Jack Dempsey

On a late Midwestern winter's day, two brothers exchanged electronic thoughts. One, a writer with unbridled passion for his home state, emailed the other, an avid reader fiercely proud of all things Michigan, seeking input on a project. "If it were written, would anyone value a biography of (a certain Michigan author)?" "Of course," came the immediate reply: the story of that author's life is rooted in the soil here, and his work would not still be in print if he hadn't been from Michigan, made his home here, and written of Michigan. Place, the brothers soon concurred, was key to the writer's legacy.

From this exchange during the season of melting snows and lengthening days, when visions of road trips revive, emerged a notion. "What about a travel guide to Michigan writer destinations?" they mused while sharing memories of family vacations across the two pleasant peninsulas. It would portray a Michigan Writer's Trail, highlighting the state's literary and travel heritage. Tourism would be a natural feature of the work, for Michigan has long been a vacationer's delight. But as to literary heritage, one could be skeptical—has the Great Lakes State spawned writing that flourished because of a Michigan origin?

As we two journeyed through time and across Michigan to find authors and places, the trip resembled a cruise along its well-worn highways and wide city streets. One writer, for example, merited statewide celebration during the fiftieth anniversary of his national bestseller. More often, though, the effort involved off-roading through unfamiliar settings that are just as genuinely Michigan as its familiar scenes. While several writers remain on the literary map, others necessitated accidental discovery. Michigan connections of others who achieved lasting fame also were pleasant revelations.

As with too much about Michigan these days, its literary heritage is underappreciated. Marked by diversity in gender and geography, fiction and nonfiction, prose and poetry, it is rich indeed. Some writing has merited Pulitzers, National Book Awards, and honorary degrees; some perched for months at the top of best-seller lists. Other books found a different kind of reader, embraced by a family tradition of passing a careworn volume down through the generations. All were fashioned by hands of artists influenced by Michigan, maddened by Michigan, heartbroken over Michigan, in love with Michigan.

I have long been in love with books, likely as long as I have been fascinated by history. As a student of the American Civil War from youth, I cherish anything written by Bruce Catton. A 1970s course at Michigan State University linked Ernest Hemingway's *The Nick Adams Stories* to reminiscences of summer weeks at Camp Michigania on Walloon Lake across from his family cabin. A career as an attorney—most recently with Dickinson Wright, a storied Detroit-based law firm—makes me fond of anything by John Voelker. These names I knew, but mapping other Michigan-author places yielded surprises. A trip to Marquette meant an encounter with *Dandelion Cottage*—and discovery back home that it was a friend's family heirloom. My Civil War library has long contained Carl Sandburg's Lincoln biography, but I had overlooked the reference in its foreword to the Chickaming Goat Farm. The Civil War—and so much more—appears in Carleton and Randall. And then there was Holling Clancy Holling . . .

I remembered his *Paddle-to-the-Sea* from a children's television show and the picture book borrowed from my Redford elementary school library. Research pointed to Holling Corners, Michigan, as his birthplace. There is no such name on any map in any era. Sleuthing with the aid of good people in Jackson County finally pinpointed the origin of a creative genius who paddled his own canoe through the Great Lakes and ultimately steered his life to America's left coast. His final wish was to be returned home to Michigan, to the tiny rural graveyard on a gently sloping hill, with a marker aptly inscribed: "Part of him lives on in his books."

The work of these authors should live on; the Michigan sources of their inspiration should be known. Each chapter of this guide confirms that we are uniquely blessed here. I am grateful for the privilege of walking the trail with these writers, and with my brother, a Michigan notable author in his own right. I gained a greater appreciation for the role of this place in shaping its literature. I have come to know better the landscapes and writing retreats of some of the state's most interesting talents. Each deserves a marker of recognition on this trail, and to be cherished for their relationship to places that are pure Michigan.

May your own journey through this guide be one of discovery and inspiration.

Southeast Michigan

George Matthew Adams

"Today's Talk"

August 23, 1878–October 28, 1962

Born in Saline; lived in several other Michigan towns

Henry Ford's Greenfield Village in Dearborn harbors the auto titan's
boyhood home, Thomas Edison's multi-invention laboratory, the Wright
Brothers' flight headquarters, George Washington Carver's childhood
cabin, Abraham Lincoln's rural courthouse, Luther Burbank's garden
studio, and Noah Webster's research center. One may still saunter down
its lamp-lit streets to discover structures representing a golden age of
nineteenth- and twentieth-century creative leadership in the United
States. The homes, businesses, and retreats of these giants are thoughtfully
arranged in the village to instill pride and inspire genius.

A sign in front of another village building identifies it as the "Adams
Family Home." On an antique table inside the narrow first-floor hallway,
single-page flyers bearing the heading "Today's Talk" are available to
peruse. Thinking them an explanation for the day's program, visitors are
surprised to find instead reprints of short articles published decades ago,
each on a single theme of some positive nature, authored by the Adams

Adams as successful writer and owner of a major publishing syndicate in New York City. Courtesy of Adventist Heritage Ministry.

for whom the house is named. This is not one of the Massachusetts Adamses (politician or brewer), or the famous nature photographer Ansel Adams, or Scott Adams, creator of the business-spoofing comic strip "Dilbert." The name of George M. Adams is given credit on these broadsides. The house is old; surely the subject matter of these slight pamphlets must no longer be relevant. For a modern e-book-buying public that cannot get enough of self-improvement guides, though, such a judgment might not be so true. When did this author live and die? How was it that he came to write such columns? Why is his home preserved in "America's greatest history attraction," a sprawling park dedicated to the creative powers of Firestone, Foster, Frost? Just what was "Today's Talk"?

George Matthew Adams was born in the parsonage of the Baptist church in Saline, Michigan, on August 23, 1878. The house was located at the southeast corner of Ann Arbor and Henry Streets, just below the main road through town. John Quincy Adams—no relative—signed the lot's first deed.

The humble parson's house in which George Matthew Adams enjoyed early childhood in Saline, now in the care of The Henry Ford in Dearborn. Photo by Jack Dempsey.

The church building stood across the street (and still does). It was a modest home, in keeping with the frugality and humble station to which ministers of the Gospel were accustomed in the late nineteenth century. A central hall divided the house into two sections, with the minister's study on the left as one entered, matched by a bedroom on the right. Five children, including George and his twin sister, necessitated the clever use of all available space.

Now a small city, subsumed in a bustling suburban Washtenaw County community of some nine thousand residents, Saline near the turn of the twentieth century was a village one-fifth that size. Its location astride the Chicago Road on the way to the Illinois metropolis made it a stopping point for weary travelers. Today, on the way westward into town, on the route that is designated US-12, one finds a large industrial facility on the north side, once a Ford Motor Company plant.

George spent his first three years at this plain house in Saline. The career of a small-town Michigan minister could involve many moves, and the Adams family relocated during the next decade to other small churches in the southern part of the state. According to the 1899 *Baptist Ministerial Directory*, the Adamses resided in Grand Rapids, Parma, Reading, Centreville, and Rochester. Most of these communities were rural, where the church building, humble as it might be, served as the lodestar for weekly experience. Despite the family's peripatetic life, George grew up confident about the future, for the words his father shared with congregants had a life-giving and sustaining power.

After the family left Michigan in 1894 for Iowa, the young man continued his education until graduating from university in Ottawa, Kansas. He moved to Chicago, megacity of many opportunities, for a career in advertising. Adams began at the bottom and worked his way up, quite literally: his first job was elevator operator. By his mid-twenties, he had graduated to writing advertising copy, which paid more but satisfied him less. He became determined to write messages of more lasting value. Thus began the authorship of daily notes, each dealing with a theme such as self-confidence, persistence, or other virtues that could encourage and motivate the reader. These messages began to make their way into newspapers and periodicals thanks to the author's connections in the industry. Before long Adams had his own column—"Today's Talk"—which gained wide appeal, appearing in *Good Housekeeping* magazine and in growing syndication across North America.

Building upon the success of his column, Adams formed a syndicate in 1907 and invited other writers to join the "Adams Newspaper Service." Its stable of contributors grew to include a diverse group, including fellow Michiganders Edna Ferber and Edgar Guest, Book-of-the-Month Club founder William Allen White, and New York City bishop Fulton J. Sheen. One of its main features was comic strips, since newspapers needed to fill small spaces with amusing material for their subscribers. The kindly humor and humble advice dispensed by these cartoons found a ready audience. Because of the expanding renown of its founder, within a decade the company was renamed the "George Matthew Adams Service" and moved from Chicago to New York City, publishing capital of the nation.

"Today's Talk" had its roots in several aspects of Adams's life. One was his time at Ottawa University, a Baptist-affiliated college whose mission had long been to further the welfare of the Ottawa Indians. Adams's own rise-to-riches story was important. His father never made much money, and the son's good fortune and fame in the publishing business inspired gratitude and a desire to share good news with the reading public. Above all, religious grounding that began in a small Saline parsonage provided the soil in which Adams nurtured a life of unflagging optimism. His writing appealed to the metaphysical needs of average Americans. His column gave them a periodic burst of hope, confidence, and energy amid the travails of the day.

Seeking to take advantage of his byline, Adams published a book of poetry in 1910 called *Uncle Walt, the Poet Philosopher*. It had modest success. Undaunted, in 1913 he authored a volume entitled *You Can*, comprising a collection of brief talks, founded on his columns, treating what it described as the most important topic in the world: "your success." The message did not necessarily focus on financial achievement; Adams sought to edify readers by picturing outcomes that would enhance their lives, promote their happiness, fulfill their dreams. One talk dealt with the topic of courage:

> Courage is naked Right put through fire and brought out uncracked and
> unbroken.
> Courage is heartworth making itself felt in deeds. It never waits for chances;
> it makes chances.

Its author betrayed a talent rooted in ad copy but striving to do more than sell merchandise.

In 1920—in the aftermath of the first worldwide bloodletting—Adams published a slim book having but a single, capitalized word for a title: *UP*. Subtitled *A Little Book of Talks on How to Wake Up, Get Up, Think Up, Climb Up, Smile Up, Cheer Up, Work Up, Look Up, Help Up, Grow Up!*, the volume did not fit any customary genre. It was not designed only to feather the pocket of its creator, for the inside cover assured the reader that "*UP* is a book to give away." Whether it had such merit can be judged from a column entitled "Hello, Rocks—Hello, Trees":

> A matchless tree waves its limbs in a mild moving wind and a note of music, more
> wonderful than any ever breathed by a harp, comes to my ear . . . The further you
> get from Nature, the less happy you are; and the nearer, the more exultant you

become over the world and all that there is in it. There is nothing unbeautiful in nature. Even the decaying tree, the dead bush, the vanishing stream—each is beautiful. If you know how to see, "all's right with the world." For everything that Nature creates is clean and right.

This was Henry Thoreau distilled for a new age. Similarly, there is the heartening theme of "Praise":

I have a wonderful business . . . I run a business which furnishes half a nation or so with something that lights up people's hearts and lives. And my biggest asset is the praise I give to the writers and artists who keep these millions in the happy zone. I love my business because it gives me the chance to praise . . . The next best thing to being praised is for you to praise. I know because I have tried it out. So don't be afraid to praise.

This may be the first incarnation of the now popular phrase "in the zone." A concluding chapter is "The Open Fireplace," and it begins with:

I write this little talk before an open fireplace. How like life it is! . . . I say to myself that I shall try to make my life like an open fireplace, so that people may be warmed and cheered by it and so go out themselves to warm and cheer.

Within the decade, the nation plummeted into the Great Depression, and Adams encountered another crisis that challenged his positive philosophy. One of those broadsides on the hallway table of the Greenfield Village house contains a passage he wrote in 1937:

People do not want what we have in our pockets half as much as they want what is in our hearts. If we combine both, intelligently, however, according to our means, we give wisely and well.

Such a sentiment might seem delusional in the midst of severe economic distress. Yet it hearkened back to a biblical principle—a lesson Adams no doubt learned from his father's sermons in small town Michigan churches: "Every work which he began he did with all his heart and prospered."

Although Adams was living in New York, a part of his heart remained in Michigan. A broadside bearing the title "Birthplaces" contains this revealing and hopeful story:

A few years ago I visited the little cottage in Michigan where I was born. It's a small story and a half frame structure that stands next to a church. I stood there and looked at it. I thought of the gentle Mother who gave me birth, with that of my sister, who is my twin. I thought of the joy and thrill it must have given to her—and I reviewed the anxieties of that time that she must have had, always wondering what sort of man I would be and what would become of her only boy . . . It is a credit to any nation or community that preserves these birthplaces . . . as an object lesson and an inspiration to the youth of today, so unacquainted with circumstances that have bequeathed to them so great an inheritance.

Henry Ford greatly admired George Matthew Adams. After driving through Saline during 1937, the same year as "give wisely and well," he determined to acquire the writer's childhood home for his history park, relocate it to Dearborn, and "restore" it to a glory it might never have seen. Ford stocked it with books by Adams and from Adams's library. After all, according to the auto magnate, Adams's writings were "so typical of the America we all love." Today, it still contains artifacts donated by the author, such as the "big, funny bed" he was born in, the coverlet his mother made him, original paintings of hers, and a book of his father's sermons in which he placed special mementos. In June 1942, he spent a night in that front bedroom as if to relive his Saline origins.

Two decades later, on October 28, 1962, coincident with the end of another national crisis, Adams died in his home in the Bronx, age eighty-four. Reporting on his funeral there, the *New York Times* obituary said of the "Today's Talk" columns: "They revealed human sympathy and cheerful optimism." It also mentioned that he had won the 1959 Freedom Foundation Award for "outstanding achievement in bringing about better understanding between peoples." In an era when the term "diversity" usually meant nothing more than a difference in opinion, Adams had been about the business of lifting up all of humanity, from the village of Saline to Greenwich Village to Greenfield Village.

Although the glory of the author's byline has faded, the pioneer frame house survives as testament to the principles upon which it and the church building across the street were built, and upon which its famous inhabitant founded his life. Life in small Michigan towns that Adams knew as the son of a minister laid the groundwork for a lifetime of positive thinking. More than a decade before Dale Carnegie published *How to Win Friends and Influence People*, and years before fellow Michigan-born Dr. Wayne Dyer became famous for offering motivational inspiration to anxious Americans, a Michigander by the well-known name of Adams was already talking the way up.

Works

* *

You Can: A Collection of Brief Talks on the Most Important Topic in the World—Your Success (New York: Frederick A. Stokes Co., 1913).

Take It: Suggestions as to Your Right to the World and the Great Things That Are in It (New York: Frederick A. Stokes Co., 1917).

UP: A Little Book of Talks on How to Wake Up, Get Up, Think Up, Climb Up, Smile Up, Cheer Up, Work Up, Look Up, Help Up, Grow Up! (Chicago: Reilly and Lee Co., 1920).

Just Among Friends (New York: W. Morrow and Co., 1928).

Better Than Gold (New York: Duell, Sloan and Pierce, 1949).

The Great Little Things (New York: Duell, Sloan and Pierce, 1953).

Sites[1]

* *

Adams Family Home at The Henry Ford (Greenfield Village), 20900 Oakwood Boulevard, Dearborn, Michigan 48124

Original Baptist church site, 117 South Ann Arbor Street, Saline, Michigan, with parsonage directly south

Kenyon, Frost, and Miller

Arbor Days

Jane Kenyon: May 23, 1947–April 22, 1995
Born in Ann Arbor Township; graduate of Ann Arbor Pioneer High School
and the University of Michigan-Ann Arbor; lived in Ann Arbor

Robert Frost: March 26, 1874–January 29, 1963
Fellow at the University of Michigan-Ann Arbor

Arthur Miller: October 17, 1915–February 10, 2005
Graduate of the University of Michigan-Ann Arbor

Neither Robert Frost nor Arthur Miller was born in Michigan. Neither lived here long, and neither died or was buried here. Jane Kenyon was born in Michigan; she lived here through college until marriage drew her away to New England. Miller returned to Michigan several times before his death in 2005; Frost came back less often after his stint in the 1920s, though descendants made the state their home. Kenyon's visits after college graduation in 1972 were sporadic. The three would seem to have little in common and literary careers little influenced by all things Michigan. The link among these poets and playwright was their tenure at the University of Michigan's campus in Ann Arbor. Miller, Frost, and Kenyon—all award winners, each with a unique talent—derived much from, and owed much to, the Great Lakes State and the college town they experienced.

Ann Arbor has a singular flavor. Although a conservative bastion for much of its existence, in the late twentieth and early twenty-first centuries it became a haven for liberal ideas and causes. Tradition says its name derives from two sources: the same first name of the wives of its founders, and the foliage tenting the Huron River that flows by campus. Ann Arbor's identity as the "city of trees" has long stood. Home to one of the nation's top universities, the community relies for half its population on students, professors, and administrative employees of the institution known as "U of M." The main site of the university is downtown, entwined within the city like an expanding vine. Farmland and green space surround the core, a thriving cultural center full of creative opportunity and energy.

Jane Kenyon was a baby boomer, born in 1947 from the union of a jazz musician and a nightclub singer. Her childhood was spent in an Ann Arbor Township house down an unpaved farm road just outside the city boundaries. When her musical parents were not performing out on the circuit, they spent considerable time in their farm garden, and Jane and her brother grew up relishing family time planting in their small patch of paradise.

Her father's mother, Dora, a native of Owosso whose childhood had been spent in a strict Methodist home, lived on State Street downtown. The kids frequently were put in their grandmother's charge, and those experiences made a deep imprint on Jane concerning things religious. Dora's approach to spirituality concentrated on the Apocalypse and eternal punishment, severe images that implanted fear and guilt in a young girl's imagination. Kenyon would later describe how the loving Savior of Scripture became transmuted into a monstrous, graying "Jesus Senior" because of a grandmother's eschatology. The emotional scarring would drive Kenyon away from her God for a long time. A childhood complicated by parental separation and an overwhelming sense of sinfulness shaped her into an introspective and insecure young woman fitted out for a lifelong struggle with depression. A poem of her youth concluded with the fear of maternal abandonment, betraying a soul in torment:

Sometimes when she goes downtown,
I think she will not come back.

Given its proximity and secularity, it was natural for Kenyon to attend U of M. Although founded as the "Catholepistemiad" of Michigan, whose

Jane Kenyon's poetry explored spiritual dimensions shaped originally by a poignant childhood rooted in the country outside of Ann Arbor. The shades of evening descended too quickly upon her life.

first president was Reverend John Montieth and vice-president was Father Gabriel Richard, the school had long grown beyond its religious roots. Kenyon earned both undergraduate (1970) and graduate (1972) degrees in English during turbulent years on campus. A war in Vietnam spawned domestic conflicts at many American colleges, and "The Harvard of the Midwest" became a fulcrum of the crisis, with protests, marches, sit-ins, teach-ins, and dropouts. Kenyon's freedom at college enabled her to rebel against the strictures of her grandmother's religion; these days of rage could have shaped her into an irreligious radical.

Jane had long enjoyed writing, as revealed by poetic fragments and regular entries in adolescent journals. Her destiny might have led her to an underground journal or on issues of international scope. Instead, she would employ herself on a far different plane. Some of the influence on her work derived from classroom time on the central campus, where Kenyon got to know English instructor Donald Hall particularly well. He was older by nearly two decades, but their discussions about writing evolved into love and marriage. Their partnership culminated a period of self-discovery that gave focus to the remainder of her life after an erratic college career.

The University of Michigan campus in central Ann Arbor, not far geographically from Kenyon's childhood home. Here she found her voice and discovered her muse. Photo by Jack Dempsey.

Kenyon's years at U of M reflected the ups and downs of a psyche in search of meaning and direction. She dropped out during her freshman year, then reenrolled as a French major after a year away, and in 1969 decided to take, somewhat as a lark, an introductory poetry class taught by Hall. Thoroughly enthralled by the subject matter, Kenyon competed for admission into the professor's fall creative-writing course and—in a huge boost to her self-confidence—was admitted on the strength of a poem, *The Needle*. It became one of the works in her first published volume. The university provided her with something she had not experienced since early youth: a close-knit community of artists, who might argue about truth and meaning, but who also loved to share. Classmates continued to associate after the semester ended, and Kenyon would regularly drop by Hall's office for a critique of her poems in progress.

Using one of those pieces, Kenyon entered a competition for the Hopwood Award. The prize was the brainchild of 1905 U of M graduate James

Avery Hopwood, who became perhaps the most successful playwright on Broadway during the 1920s. One of the nation's oldest and largest award programs, the Hopwood outweighed in prestige its small stipend and brought a sense of validation to its recipients. Winning an award in 1969 thrilled Kenyon and validated her desire to be a writer. Far from taking on world affairs, Kenyon decided to concentrate on the individual challenges in life— the conflicts and emotions that flesh out a person's existence. Her work would deal with "macro" issues, yes, but on a "micro" scale, exploring truth in the inner sanctum, through the power of spare verse.

The first several years of the marriage were spent in the friendly confines of Ann Arbor. Although the couple would take up more permanent residence in New Hampshire, the rural settings in many of her poems hearken to the fields and farms she knew surrounding the university town. Like many exurban Detroit communities, Ann Arbor experienced steady expansion that ended up consuming the rural setting of her girlhood. Their move to a farm in New England restored the pastoral world to Kenyon—one might say it helped get her back to the garden. Nature became a frequent subject in her poems, rebuilding her relationship with its creator from the days of childhood innocence. Kenyon rediscovered a God whose face shone upon her with a warmth that overshadowed the hard images cultivated by her grandmother.

That spiritual reawakening became vital when Kenyon was stricken in her mid-forties with leukemia. She contended with the disease in her poetry and in her life, until realizing, and accepting, that it would not be conquered. Kenyon was not consumed by her approaching death, but she grieved for the truncating of a happy life with Hall and the work that remained. It helped inspire some of her greatest writing. Awareness of mortality was never far away, as in "Let Evening Come:":

Let the light of late afternoon
shine through chinks in the barn, moving
up the bales as the sun moves down.

Let the cricket take up chafing
as a woman takes up her needles
and her yarn. Let evening come.

Let dew collect on the hoe abandoned
in long grass. Let the stars appear
and the moon disclose her silver horn.

Let the fox go back to its sandy den.
Let the wind die down. Let the shed
go black inside. Let evening come.

To the bottle in the ditch, to the scoop
in the oats, to air in the lung
let evening come.

Let it come, as it will, and don't
be afraid. God does not leave us
comfortless, so let evening come.

An excerpt is inscribed on a marker on Evening Island overlooking an appropriately tranquil setting at the famed Chicago Botanic Garden. "Notes from the Other Side," in less than a hundred words, said everything about Kenyon's state of faith:

I divested myself of despair and fear when I came here.
Now there is no more catching one's own eye in the mirror,
there are no more bad books, no plastic, no insurance premiums, and of course,
no illness. Contrition does not exist, nor gnashing
of teeth. No one howls as the first clod of earth hits the casket.
The poor we no longer have with us. Our calm hearts strike only the hour,
and God, as promised, proves to be mercy clothed in light.

Her battle ended at the premature age of forty-seven. She was buried in Proctor Cemetery in Andover, New Hampshire, in the state that had declared her its poet laureate.

Despite an output of only four books during her lifetime, containing characteristically lean yet evocative poetry, Kenyon's work received high acclaim during and afterward. An untimely death could have consigned her writing to oblivion. Not the case, for the *New York Times* hailed how "these poems surprise beauty at every turn" and are "deep, transparent and luminous."

Other reviewers agreed: "Rare among American poets, she is also able to infuse her poetry with a lightly worn sense of Christian humility, and an active—if worried—sense of mercy. These are among the qualities which give her verse both the tones and the turns of serious prayer."[1] "Her words, with their quiet, rapt force, their pensiveness and wit, come to us from natural speech, from the Bible and hymns, from which she derived the singular psalmlike music that is hers alone."[2] Her "memorable poems trace the channels of extraordinary spiritual trials and the measured redemptions of an extraordinary imagination."[3]

Those psalms embody the Kenyon paradox: Is God fearsome or friend? Her youth in Ann Arbor on a farm, in a grandparent's house, and on a college campus all contributed to a poetry both of pathos and of contentment. Evening came for Jane Kenyon too soon; it should not come for her work.

Robert Lee Frost, likely the best-known American poet, early on led a peripatetic life. Born in California and named after the Civil War general, Frost moved as a boy to Massachusetts with his mother, upon his father's death. He spent much of his life in the New England states but frequently wintered in Florida. On one occasion, escaping responsibility involved fleeing to the Great Dismal Swamp on the Virginia/North Carolina border. On another, escaping the prospect of failure meant a sojourn in England. Early on he was not confident of his standing.

Frost's later reputation as the greatest American poet of the twentieth century—arising from four Pulitzers, numerous accolades, and over forty honorary degrees—is linked to an image of a solitary, wizened writer with pencil in hand, deep in thought in his Vermont farm studio, seeking inspiration from a snowy landscape of rocks and trees under an overcast New England sky. Not many would imagine that he often spent winters in tropical climes. None would likely couple Frost with the Midwest. His last major public appearance, at the inauguration of John F. Kennedy, exposed a feeble gray-haired man, forced to recite an older work when blinding sunlight disabled him from reading the composition he had created for the event. For many, the idea of a youthful Robert Frost would seem incongruously laughable. Yet, when he alighted from the Michigan Central train at the Ann Arbor

Robert Frost in the era of his fellowship at the University of Michigan. Here he wrote such classic poems as "Spring Pools" to portray Michigan's flowery waters, forests and woods, and reflected sky. Courtesy of the Bentley Historical Library, University of Michigan.

depot in October 1921, a successful poet still growing in critical stature, his vigor did not differ much from that of the students he was brought west to mentor.

Frost's rail ride came after Marion L. Burton, president of the University of Michigan, made him an attractive offer. Supporting himself as a farmer in New Hampshire and on the lecture circuit took precious time away from writing. Former Michigan governor and U of M regent Chase Osborn had agreed to sponsor Frost as the university's first "fellow of the arts" with a $5,000 stipend, a huge sum in those days and even more than Frost had sought for such a post. The deal was sealed by an immediately penciled approval from Frost. He would teach no classes and had no specific office hours or duties. The fellowship was open-ended: the poet would mingle with creative arts students, inspire them, help them to write, nurture their muse. It succeeded for both teacher and student.

It worked so well, in fact, that Frost was brought back for a second stint in 1922, this time through the generosity of Horace Rackham, one of Ford Motor Company's original shareholders. Frost's work that session included arranging a poets' lectureship at which Carl Sandburg and other literary luminaries spoke. Not all such occasions were auspicious. Local poet Edgar A. Guest was the other guest of honor at one dinner party; Frost did not regard it as a meeting of equals. Although this second term was regarded as less beneficial, the university offered him a position in 1925 teaching a seminar for students with particular promise. President Burton—for whom a landmark tower on campus is named—became chief cheerleader of a lifetime appointment as Fellow in Letters. Burton's untimely death, after Frost had accepted, undermined the arrangement. Instead, Frost ended up parlaying the offer into a position back in New England, where his family preferred to live.

During his fellowship years, the Frosts resided in a one-and-a-half story Greek Revival home at 1223 Pontiac Road (now Trail), at the corner of Kellogg Street north of town. It was designed in a style Frost called "hen and chicks." The comfortable setting enabled him to employ creativity in his own work as well as in aiding students. Here he composed several memorable poems. One, "Spring Pools," suggested the landscape in the tree-filled environs of Ann Arbor:

> These pools that, though in forests, still reflect
> The total sky almost without defect,
> And like the flowers beside them, chill and shiver,
> Will like the flowers beside them soon be gone,
> And yet not out by any brook or river,
> But up by roots to bring dark foliage on.
> The trees that have it in their pent-up buds
> To darken nature and be summer woods—
> Let them think twice before they use their powers
> To blot out and drink up and sweep away
> These flowery waters and these watery flowers
> From snow that melted only yesterday.

Other poems with Michigan roots included "Acquainted with the Night," "A Winter Eden" (describing "a winter garden in an alder swamp," a not unfamiliar scene in Northern Michigan), "A Minor Bird," "What Fifty Said," and "The Nose Ring." In dedicating his Pulitzer-winning book of poems entitled

The "hen and chicks" home once inhabited by Robert Frost and family in Ann Arbor is now preserved at The Henry Ford in Dearborn. Photo by Jack Dempsey.

New Hampshire, Frost gave credit for its inspiration to Michigan, since it was where he had done so much of the writing.

And there was this little piece of work penned in the hen-and-chicks house:

Whose woods these are I think I know.
His house is in the village though;
He will not see me stopping here
To watch his woods fill up with snow.
My little horse must think it queer
To stop without a farmhouse near
Between the woods and frozen lake
The darkest evening of the year.
He gives his harness bells a shake
To ask if there is some mistake.
The only other sound's the sweep
Of easy wind and downy flake.

The woods are lovely, dark and deep.
But I have promises to keep,
And miles to go before I sleep,
And miles to go before I sleep.

The final, echoing line, one of the most famous in American verse, concluded "Stopping by Woods on a Snowy Evening"—a wintry setting that matched the Southeast Michigan landscape Frost enjoyed during his tenure.

"I like Michigan people and I like Michigan," Frost revealed later, confessing to have become "a good deal more Ann Arboreal than I should suppose I could have at my age." He returned several times to the university that had helped make him a central figure in letters, as early as 1927 and as late as a special convocation in April 1962, less than a year before his death. His remarks to an overflow audience at the final Hill Auditorium gathering were retrospective, recalling the friendship with Burton and associations with students. It was at Michigan that he identified several favored female students as his "three graces." And he admitted "a lot of the outlying landscape" had been "pretty well incorporated" in his consciousness. He recalled the Pontiac Trail home with warmth: "It was a very pretty little thing made altogether out of black walnut . . . a very pretty little house . . . a very charming house." Here he had enjoyed "poetic teas by the fire" and reviewing the work of budding student poets.

After a series of heart episodes, Frost died on January 29, 1963, and was buried in the Old Cemetery in Bennington, Vermont. The *New York Times* obituary described him as a symbol of "the rough-hewn individuality of the American creative spirit more than any other man." The newspaper did not credit his reputation to time in the Midwest; it was just as well. Frost's reminiscences during that final Ann Arbor appearance suggested a softer spirit, one who had found its community and its environs to be nurturing.

A decade after Frost's descent from the train at the Ann Arbor depot, a six-foot-tall, hard-working young man graduated from Abraham Lincoln High in Brooklyn, New York. His teachers and friends noted him much more for athletic than scholastic abilities. Although Arthur Miller's father once had been wealthy enough to afford a chauffeur, the stock market crash of 1929 knocked the family down several financial notches. Now that a more prestigious college was out of reach, Miller clung to the slim reed of one contingency: according to a neighbor attending the University of Michigan, the Ann Arbor college was a possibility he should explore. After all, tuition was a mere $65 per semester.

Miller unsuccessfully submitted two applications before abandoning procedure and resorting to a plea for admission, in a plaintive letter, directly to the dean. He was conditionally accepted, based on showing proof of enough savings to afford both attendance and a place to live. A better part of a year passed before he had accumulated the necessary funds. While commuting via subway to the job that made college possible, Miller used the time to read and substitute his penchant for popular fiction with classics. This preparatory work inspired him to think about a career in writing.

Miller entered the university in the fall of 1934 as a journalism major. He reported for the *Michigan Daily*, gaining valuable writing experience. One of the events he covered was the now-famous sit-down strike at a Flint General Motors plant. Moving up a notch to be the paper's night editor brought with it a small salary and the prospect of extending his studies. No financial support came from home; he had to survive with odd jobs, such as washing dishes in exchange for meals at an Ann Arbor co-op, and walking several miles each day to a position taking care of lab rats for $15 a month.

Financial straits led him to pore through the U of M catalog to find ways to make ends meet. The Hopwood Award was one possibility. He spent a spring break writing a play, *No Villain*, which he entered in the competition hoping that lightning might strike. It did, producing a $250 award. The play was given an amateur production at the Lyric Mendelssohn Theatre in Ann Arbor. Though the money and exposure were important, the main benefit was a confidence it inspired to change Miller's major to English. The new curriculum would enable him to concentrate on his new love: playwriting. He won a scholarship to study with Kenneth Thorpe Rowe, noted U of M drama professor. Miller won a second Hopwood in 1937 for *Honors at Dawn*, and a second-place prize in 1938. By the time he graduated that year, he had met his wife, demonstrated a proven talent for playwriting, and gained a staunch ally in Professor Rowe.

Returning to New York City, Miller took along a letter of recommendation from Rowe to the Federal Theater Project, a Depression-era government

Arthur Miller came to Michigan from New York City because of the University of Michigan's playwriting curriculum and generous application of its admissions policy. The campus is home to the only theater he authorized to wear his name. Courtesy of the Bentley Historical Library, University of Michigan.

program similar to the CCC, WPA, and Federal Writers' Project. His credentials, and Rowe's endorsement, got him in. Joining it enabled him to launch a career as a playwright, but he sold very little at first. His wife, Mary Slattery, opened doors for him through her position as an editor at Harper and Brothers. In 1947 his play *All My Sons*, whose protagonist, Joe Keller, was a prototypical Midwesterner, achieved a level of success he had coveted. It ran for over three hundred performances, garnering awards—including best play of the season by the Drama Critics' Circle—and many favorable reviews, establishing Miller's reputation as a serious dramatist specializing in tragic storylines.

Just two years later, Miller hit the big time. The soon-to-be-classic *Death of a Salesman* premiered to universal acclaim—one critic called it "emotional dynamite"—and it won the Pulitzer Prize, among numerous awards. The play made history as the first of its genre to become a Book-of-the-Month Club selection. *Death* told the story of Willie Loman, a traveling salesman desperately failing at life, whose tragic end brought audiences to tears. The play was full of affecting speeches, such as "A man can't go out the

The boarding house in Ann Arbor where Miller billeted while a college student. Here he wrote plays that won him two Hopwood designations. Photo by Jack Dempsey.

way he came in, Ben, a man has got to add up to something." The author's life embodied the line.

Miller also wrote *The Crucible*, a standard text in American literature classes about the Salem witch trials, and the plays *A View from the Bridge* and *Broken Glass*. His writing also made its way into numerous other genres, from short stories to books. Miller's fame as a writer was almost surpassed during the late 1950s by a short-lived marriage to actress Marilyn Monroe. Upon his death in 2005 at the age of eighty-nine, however, Miller's reputation as the greatest modern American playwright was solidly entrenched.

Arthur Miller's connections to Michigan lasted much of his lifetime. He had been attracted to U of M because "tuition was cheap—about $60, I think—and I'd heard they gave Hopwood awards to student writers. For a 19-year-old who knew he wanted to write, even though I didn't know what I'd write, the fact that the University gave a dollar prize meant they took writing seriously here." It was, he maintained, the only American university offering an intensive playwriting course where a writer could win a prize for his craft. Awarded an honorary doctorate by U of M in 1956, he later consented to the use of his name for a university theater. The approval came via postcard: "The theatre is a lovely idea. I've resisted similar proposals from others, but it seems right from Ann Arbor." The venue, the only theatre to bear his name, opened in 2007, just two years after his burial in the Center Cemetery in Roxbury, Connecticut.

As it turned out, then, the final resting place of all three Wolverines was New England.

In his autobiography, *Timebends*, Miller wrote that U of M was "a place full of speeches, meetings and leaflets. It was jumping with issues . . . political facts of life were not all I learned. I learned that under certain atmospheric conditions, you could ice skate up and down all the streets in Ann Arbor at night." The campus "was very welcoming and I found it a very good environment for mixing with a lot of people I normally wouldn't have met." "It was my idea of what a university should be," he wrote a couple of decades after his graduation. "It helped to lay out the boundaries of my life."

In 1985, the Hopwood-winning playwright established an award in his own name to provide financial aid to Michigan students and help inspire them to become the next successful playwright, echoing the key support he had received as a young man. Similarly, Robert Frost lent his name to initiatives at the institution after his midlife sojourn, paving the way for the creation of several archival collections relating to his life and work. Death prevented dual Hopwood recipient Jane Kenyon from paying it back to U of M. All of them, however, evidenced how formative years spent on the campus of Michigan's oldest collegiate training ground contributed to their writing careers. One of them came as a teacher, two as students. Each discovered a wellspring of inspiration. During different eras, as the tree-shaded streets of Ann Arbor moved through their seasons, the three found in Michigan a special place.

Works

. . . .

JANE KENYON
From Room to Room (Cambridge, MA: Alice James Books, 1978).
The Boat of Quiet Hours (St. Paul, MN: Graywolf Press, 1986).
Let Evening Come (St. Paul, MN: Graywolf Press, 1990).
Constance (St. Paul, MN: Graywolf Press, 1993).
Otherwise: New and Selected Poems (St. Paul, MN: Graywolf Press, 1996).

A Hundred White Daffodils (St. Paul, MN: Graywolf Press, 1999).

Jane Kenyon: Collected Poems (St. Paul, MN: Graywolf Press, 2005.

ROBERT FROST

A Boy's Will (London: David Nutt, 1913).

North of Boston (London: David Nutt, 1914).

Mountain Interval (New York: Henry Holt and Co., 1916).

Selected Poems (New York: Henry Holt and Co., 1923).

New Hampshire (New York: Henry Holt and Co., 1923).

Several Short Poems (New York: Henry Holt and Co., 1924).

Selected Poems (New York: Henry Holt and Co., 1928).

West-Running Brook (New York: Henry Holt and Co., 1929).

The Lovely Shall Be Choosers (New York: Random House, 1929).

A Way Out: A One Act Play (New York: Harbor Press, 1929).

The Cow's in the Corn: A One Act Irish Play in Rhyme (Gaylordsville, CT: Slide Mountain Press, 1929).

Collected Poems of Robert Frost (New York: Henry Holt and Co., 1930).

The Lone Striker (New York: Alfred A. Knopf, 1933).

Selected Poems: Third Edition (New York: Henry Holt and Co., 1934).

Three Poems (Hanover, NH: Baker Library, Dartmouth College, 1935).

The Gold Hesperides (Cortland, NY: Bibliophile Press, 1935).

From Snow to Snow (New York: Henry Holt and Co., 1936).

A Further Range (New York: Henry Holt and Co., 1936).

Collected Poems of Robert Frost (New York: Henry Holt and Co., 1939).

A Witness Tree (New York: Henry Holt and Co., 1942).

A Masque of Reason (New York: Henry Holt and Co., 1945) [play].

Steeple Bush (New York: Henry Holt and Co., 1947).

A Masque of Mercy (New York: Henry Holt and Co., 1947) [play].

Complete Poems of Robert Frost, 1949 (New York: Henry Holt and Co., 1949).

Hard Not to Be King (New York: House of Books, 1951).

Aforesaid (New York: Henry Holt and Co., 1954).

A Remembrance Collection of New Poems (New York: Henry Holt and Co., 1959).

You Come Too (New York: Henry Holt and Co., 1959).

In the Clearing (New York: Holt, Rinehart & Winston, 1962).

Situation Normal (New York: Reynal & Hitchcock, 1944).

Focus (New York: Reynal & Hitchcock, 1945).

All My Sons (New York: Reynal & Hitchcock, 1947).

Death of a Salesman (New York: Viking Press, 1949).

An Enemy of the People (adapted from Henrik Ibsen's play) (New York: Viking Press, 1951).

The Crucible (New York: Viking Press, 1953; Bantam, 1959).

A View from the Bridge: A Play in Two Acts (New York: Viking Press, 1957).

The Misfits (London: Secker & Warburg, 1961).

Jane's Blanket (New York: Crowell-Collier Press, 1963).

After the Fall (New York: Viking Press, 1964).

Incident at Vichy (New York: Viking Press, 1965).

I Don't Need You Anymore: Stories (New York: Viking Press, 1967).

The Price (London: Secker & Warburg, 1968; New York: Viking Press, 1968).

In Russia (with Inge Morath) (New York: Viking Press, 1969).

Poetry and Film: Two Symposiums (with Dylan Thomas) (New York: Gotham Book Mart, 1972).

The Creation of the World and Other Business (New York: Viking Press, 1973).

In the Country (with Inge Morath) (New York: Viking Press, 1977).

The Theater Essays of Arthur Miller (New York: Viking Press, 1978).

Chinese Encounters (with Inge Morath) (New York: Farrar, Straus & Giroux, 1979).

Playing for Time (New York: Bantam Books, 1981).

The American Clock (adapted from Studs Terkel's *Hard Times*) (New York: Dramatists Play Service, 1981).

Final Edition (New York: Pinnacle Books, 1981).

Elegy for a Lady (New York: Dramatists Play Service, 1982).

Some Kind of Love Story (New York: Dramatists Play Service, 1983).

A Memory of Two Mondays: Play in One Act (New York: Dramatists Play Service, 1983).

Up from Paradise (New York: Samuel French, 1984).

Salesman in Beijing (New York: Viking Press, 1984).

The Archbishop's Ceiling (New York: Dramatists Play Service, 1985).

Danger: Memory!: A Double-Bill of "I Can't Remember Anything" *and* "Clara" (London: Methuen, 1986).

Timebends: A Life (New York: Grove Press, 1987).

The Golden Years (London: Methuen, 1989).

Everybody Wins: A Screenplay (New York: Grove Weidenfeld, 1990).

The Last Yankee (New York: Dramatists Play Service, 1991).

Ride down Mount Morgan (New York: Penguin Books, 1992).

Homely Girl: A Life (New York: Viking Books, 1992).

Broken Glass (New York: Penguin Books, 1994).

Mr. Peter's Connections (New York: Penguin Books, 1999).

The Misfits: Story of a Shoot (with Serge Toubiana) (New York: Phaidon Press, 2000).

Sites

JANE KENYON

Newport Road north of M-14, south of Barton Pond, Ann Arbor, Michigan

ROBERT FROST

Robert Frost Home, The Henry Ford (at Greenfield Village), 20900 Oakwood Boulevard, Dearborn, Michigan 48124

ARTHUR MILLER

Arthur Miller Theater, The University of Michigan, 1226 Murfin Avenue, Ann Arbor, Michigan 48109

Rooming house, 411 North State Street, Ann Arbor, Michigan

Dudley Felker Randall

Urban Trailblazer

January 14, 1914–August 5, 2000

Lived in Detroit; graduate of Eastern High School; degrees from Wayne State University and the University of Michigan-Ann Arbor; founded Detroit-based Broadside Press

Detroit is grit. Detroit is a fast-coursing river that never slows below its surface. Detroit is a vacant building once graced by Tiffany ceilings and Pewabic tiles. Detroit is an arena's throaty roar of thousands of unified celebratory voices arising out of toughest ghetto and toniest suburb. Detroit is a main avenue that divides the city into separate cultures, east versus west. Detroit is a conductor's joyous baton and a bus driver's weary sigh. Detroit is all promise and futility and determination.

Detroit is also seen in a postal clerk who was a poet. Dudley Felker Randall was born in Washington, D.C., but became a Detroiter at the age of six. Most of the rest of his life would reflect a mainstream Detroiter experience, not the rarefied top of its economic heap. After service in World War II, he secured two degrees: one in English from Wayne State University, and the second in library science from the University of Michigan in Ann Arbor. He found work as a librarian at several out-of-state locations,

29

Dudley Randall working away at his desk at Broadside Press, circa 1981. He may be fashioning a poem; he might be editing someone else's work. Photo by Hugh Grannum.

coming home to Detroit in 1956, for good, to work in the Wayne County library system. Eventually, his abilities secured him a position as librarian at the University of Detroit, where his love for writing could freely play out.

Randall's first published poem appeared when he was thirteen, in a 1927 edition of the *Detroit Free Press*, one of several major Detroit newspapers. His poetry arose from the humble surroundings he experienced as a child of the Great Depression in urban America. Although he had graduated from Eastern High School at age sixteen, the economic hardships of the era made it impossible to achieve the dream of going to college. His family took in boarders to make ends meet, and out of the experience would come a poem, "For Pharish Pinckney, Bindle-Stiff During the Depression."[1]

The Motor City was far from integrated, but like many Detroiters, his next career move was to go into an auto plant and work on the line, an opportunity for African Americans not available in other parts of the country. And like many of his generation, he enlisted during the Second World War and served in the Pacific Theater. The experience led him to pen pieces like "Pacific Epitaphs," a multi-battle set of vignettes about soldiers and their fates, evocative of the sacrifice of those who march off to war:

Your forehead capped with steel
Is smoother than a coin
With profile of a boy who fell
At Marathon.

In "Memorial Wreath," also written while in the service, he extolled the heroism of forebears who fought for freedom in the American Civil War:

In the green month when resurrected flowers
Like laughing children ignorant of death,
Brighten the couch of those who wake no more,
Love and remembrance blossom in our hearts,
For you who bore the extreme sharp pang for us,
And bought our freedom with your lives.
...
American earth is richer for your bones:
Our hearts beat prouder for the blood we inherit.

To honor them, "violets bluer than cool northern skies" would be strewn on their graves. These are words from someone who knew firsthand about courage under fire.

Randall continued to write after being discharged, and authored a poem in 1952 reflecting a dialogue between Booker T. Washington and W.E.B. Du Bois. In point-counterpoint style, the famous leaders argued their competing points of view on how black people could thrive in America. A decade later, Randall's muse inspired a far different dialogue. Spurred by the tragic death of children in the 1963 bombing of an Alabama church building, Randall penned the haunting "Ballad of Birmingham." A mother tells a daughter who wants to march for freedom that she is too young to enter the struggle:

". . . But you may go to church instead
And sing in the children's choir."
She has combed and brushed her night-dark hair,
And bathed rose petal sweet,
And drawn white gloves on her small brown hands,
And white shoes on her feet.

The poem ends as one of those small shoes is found by the mother in the rubble of the bombed structure. Randall evoked a Christ-like parallel in the anointing of the child for burial in her favorite white apparel, juxtaposed with the immorality of the murderous white supremacists.

When a folk singer set "Ballad" to music, Randall wondered if he could maintain rights to his work. Learning that a leaflet could be copyrighted, he decided to publish it in the form of a single sheet, a broadside. A second poem found the same interest, and it, too, was broadsided. Randall had found an economical publishing medium that would serve his interest in writing as more of a career.

The civil rights movement of the 1960s helped Randall develop a vision of wider publication. Finding it insufficiently rewarding to pen his works alone, Randall opened a door for others who had no outlet. In 1965, using twelve dollars from his own pocket, he founded Broadside Press—an apt name, for the mission was to publish those single-sided leaflets, each containing a work by a person of color, producing income for them through affordable pricing, yielding additional rewards by disseminating words to a public hungry for voices that had not been heard. "We are a nation of twenty-two million souls," he wrote in 1975 about black Americans, "larger than Athens in the Age of Pericles or England in the age of Elizabeth." We should create, he wrote, "a literature which will be to our own nation what those literatures were to theirs." Literature was married with artwork, for many of the sheets were illustrated and suitable for framing.

Although "Ballad" was the first to be issued, priced at a half dollar, Randall's broader vision reached its fulfillment when works by other writers were published—such as *From a Land Where Other People Live* (Audre Lorde), which received the acclaim of a National Book Award. Gwendolyn Brooks, good friend and Pulitzer winner, moved from a major publishing house to Randall's shop. The press deliberately priced its works inexpensively and thus made them available to a wide audience of all economic means, in the Detroit area and beyond. Its success also depended on creating a network of distributors separate from the established publishing houses that traditionally had rejected the works of black Americans. Such achievements prompted one commentator to rank Broadside's contributions more highly than anything on either coast: "No other American city can match the record created in Detroit by Dudley Randall and the Broadside Press."[2]

The Randall home in Detroit, betraying the ravages of time and societal change since last occupied by the poet and his family. Photo by Jack Dempsey.

Only after the tensions of the 1960s dissipated did academia come to realize the vein of gold that could be mined from the press's output. Its founder received a Lifetime Achievement Award in 1996 from the National Endowment for the Arts for contributions to American writing. He received the first Poet Laureate award from the City of Detroit in 1981, bestowed in a ceremony by the first African American mayor of the municipality.

Such achievements are all the more amazing since, early on, the press was a one-man operation. Working out of a spare bedroom in his first home— much of which was built by his own hands—Randall read manuscripts, planned and designed the publications (soon to include books), packed shipping boxes, addressed envelopes and shipping labels, licked stamps, and did all of the other necessary activities to issue published writings on a professional level. From these modest origins grew a publishing house that produced the Broadside Critics Series of literary criticism, the Broadside Voices Series of recorded readings and performances, political analyses, cooking titles, posters, children's books, and teleplays. One critic hailed this evolution: "Broadside Press grew into one of the world's finest literary collections, with over one hundred titles, most of which were poetry." One of his authors enjoyed over 80,000 books of poetry in circulation. All in all, the press issued over a half-million books between 1965 and 1977.

The press became more than a single person could handle. Twice Randall stepped away and let someone take over who could keep the publishing house alive and well. He took it back after a period of depression and recovery, relinquishing it permanently when convinced it could last without his watchful eye. It remains alive, still independent from the large houses that rejected Randall's submissions over a half century ago. As a beacon that continues to shine, in his words and in those of others, it still issues works from a location in the New Center area of Detroit, carrying on the legacy of one of Michigan's literary trailblazers.

Wayne State University, where Randall worked for many years, honored him in 2000 by establishing the Dudley Randall Center for Print Culture. At its founding, the institution said: "The naming of the Center after Dudley Randall reflects not only our great respect for a poet and a publisher who literally transformed the face of American Literature, but also, our commitment to continuing his vision of the written word as a living art form intimately connected to community and to self-determination; as well as our commitment to continuing his vision of publishing as a vehicle for building relationships and for promoting cultural critique. Dudley Randall was a great inspiration to generations of writers, readers, and community activists. We are proud to join the other individuals and institutions that are continuing his legacy."

And so the legacy lives on. A legacy of an independent press that launched careers of many voices that would have never been heard otherwise. A legacy of a man who has been called "the other Barry Gordy," invoking the parallel career of the Motown Records founder who gave expression to the musical poetry of the African American community. Like the music company president, Randall also created lasting works.

Critics commented: "A distinctive style is difficult to identify in Randall's poetry," but it is marked by "freedom, originality, and depth of feeling." He was called "one of the foremost voices in African American literature during the twentieth century" due to his "skill as a wordsmith and his affinity for themes of love, human contradictions, and political action." Fortune, however, did not find him. Randall had to be content with rewards that promoted pride rather than expanded bank accounts. This was not a problem fundamentally, for Dudley Randall was a kind man, a Detroiter who spoke for the people, who sought not balance-sheet wealth, but the beauty of the written word.

Unlike many of Michigan's authors, Randall grew up and discovered his muse from city living. He first expressed that inspiration in poetry, following in the centuries-old oral tradition of his forebears on the African continent. Regarded by one source as "father of the black poetry movement," clearly a leader in the "Black Arts" culture that reached a zenith in the latter half of the twentieth century, Randall found expression for himself and for many others who might never have been heard without his help.

Works

. . . .

Poem Counterpoem (Detroit: Broadside Press, 1966).
Cities Burning (Detroit: Broadside Press, 1968).
Black Poetry: A Supplement to Anthologies Which Exclude Black Poets (Detroit: Broadside Press, 1969).
Love You (Detroit: Broadside Press, 1970).
More to Remember: Poems of Four Decades (Chicago: Third World Press, 1971).
After the Killing (Chicago: Third World Press, 1973).
Broadside Memories: Poets I Have Known (Detroit: Broadside Press, 1975).
A Litany of Friends: New and Selected Poems (Detroit: Lotus Press, 1981, 1983).
Roses and Revolutions: The Selected Writings of Dudley Randall (Detroit: Wayne State University Press, 2009).

Sites

. . . .

Broadside Press office, 440 Burroughs, Suite 124, Detroit, Michigan 48224
Elmwood Cemetery, 1200 Elmwood Avenue, Detroit, Michigan 48207
Home at 12651 Old Mill Place, Detroit, Michigan (near Livernois and Fenkell)

Central/South Central Michigan

William McKendree Carleton

Verse Virtuoso

October 21, 1845–December 18, 1912

Born in Hudson; attended Hillsdale College; Will Carleton Day declared by Michigan Legislature

. . . .

Draw up the papers, lawyer, and make 'em good and stout;

For things at home are crossways, and Betsey and I are out.

Contemporary song lyric? Not even close, though the notion certainly fits with today's cultural trends. It is, rather, a stanza from one of the most renowned works by Michigan's first lyricist and poet laureate, a writer whose fame lingered over a half century past his death.

Poetry once was a mainstay of American life. From Longfellow to Poe to Whitman to Dickinson, authors of verse captured the American imagination more powerfully than prose. In 1996, April was designated National Poetry Month. The genre may be making a comeback, what with poetry "slams" and hip-hop rhymes appealing to a younger generation enamored with performance art. One might even regard song lyrics as the modern substitute for readings that famed poets once gave from their works to crowds in cities and towns across this land.

Carleton, the "farmer's poet," captivated audiences across the land with lyrical readings extolling the values of rural America. Courtesy of the Bentley Historical Library, University of Michigan.

During the early nineteenth century, American verse helped bind its communities together. The era saw the Great Migration from the Eastern Seaboard through the Erie Canal and Ohio Valley into the Midwest. It was a time when most settlers bypassed Michigan's Lower Peninsula because of popular wisdom that its swamps and bogs could never become farm country. This common understanding proved uncommonly wrong. The stretch of land from the western edge of Lake Erie to the southeastern shore of Lake Michigan proved to be, for those with the temerity to settle it, supremely fecund farmland. The southern tier of counties bordering Ohio emerged as the breadbasket of Michigan during the two decades before the American Civil War.

In 1830, New England native John Hancock Carleton emigrated to Michigan like many others from the Northeast. Michigan was not yet a state, and Carleton settled first in Plymouth before relocating to the village of Hudson, then called Lanesville, in Lenawee County. It was one of the border jurisdictions with very few settlers, and Carleton staked out a pioneer farmstead two miles east of the village on the main road to Adrian. According to an early history, the family embarked upon this intra-territory journey on a Monday morning, aboard a wagon drawn by horses and oxen, and they arrived on the following Sunday—requiring six days to traverse less than ninety miles. Farmer Carleton began clearing a place on which to live, and within a week had built a log cabin 18-feet square. This early account also described the land as heavily timbered, necessitating back-breaking labor to fell the forest. Carving 60 acres from this virgin tract, Carleton cleared land and began growing crops. Native Americans, still resident in the area, called at the cabin and exchanged goods. Carleton treated them with charity, for he had brought from New England certain convictions. He was an antislavery man, one of the few abolitionists in his locale.

The log house became home to his wife Celestia and five children, including a son named William McKendree, the youngest child, born on October 21, 1845. As a boy, Will wrote his first poem, "The Dying Indian Chief." No doubt, visits to his home by the region's indigenous peoples caught the boy's imagination.

Farm work was hard, and poetry was a bit of luxury in a farmer's household in 1850s Michigan. The standard of living for most Michiganders was tied inexorably to the weather. Some 85 percent of the population engaged in livelihoods related to agriculture. Young Will Carleton could be expected to take over his father's place and spend a lifetime as a farmer, contend with fate as a farmer, and die as a farmer. There was this small matter, though, of a one-room schoolhouse near the corner of the family farm. It was there, on a daily basis—and weekly in the Methodist church in the village—that the boy found the power of words overmatched the pull of the field.

Religion was an integral force in the Carleton family. In the cadence of the King James Bible and in daily schoolhouse readings, Will came to an understanding of how and why he had been made. He no longer regarded a plowed field full of seed for a later harvest as his destiny; he began to produce a different crop with paper and pen. After graduating from the one-room schoolhouse, his interest led him west to the nearby town of Hillsdale. A college had been founded there on the principle of social equality, and it felt much like his father's house. He frequently made the trip to Hillsdale and back aboard the local train until graduation in 1869. His father expected him to return home to take up the plow, but Will's first postgraduate employment was elsewhere.

During four college years, Will Carleton had been contributing items to newspapers. A career in journalism continued at Chicago's *Western Rural*, the *Hillsdale Standard*, and Detroit's *Weekly Tribune*, where he served as writer and editor. The career choice gave him time and freedom to write more than the customary stuff; as he had since a boy, Carleton worked at verse until he felt it virtuous enough to share with others. One such piece, concerning marital difficulties, found its way into a Toledo newspaper. As was the practice then, other publications would reprint such work, providing at least attribution, if not financial compensation. And so the work came across the desk of an editor at the nationally distributed *Harper's Weekly*.

Published in 1871 when Will Carleton was only twenty-five, the piece "Betsey and I Are Out" became a springboard to fame. *Harper's* was one of the two great national publications, and it featured the poignant story of divorce and loss on its front page. The selection received huge acclaim. It had an unusual tenor—no betrayal or violence, only the story of a couple growing apart "for years, a little at a time." Their differences irreconcilable ("If I can't live kind with a woman, why, then, I won't at all"), in an era averse to divorce the two came to a lamented but mutual decision: "We have agreed together that we can't never agree." The command: "Write it on the paper, lawyer—the very first paragraph—Of all the farm and livestock that she shall have her half," for "it's nothing more then [sic] justice that Betsy has her pay." The poem ended without malice, only wistfulness:

> And one thing put in the paper, that first to me didn't occur;
> That when I'm dead at last she'll bring me back to her;
> And lay me under the maples I planted years ago,
> When she and I were happy before we quarreled so.

The door opened to more such efforts; a year later *Harper's* publication of "Over the Hill to the Poor House" confirmed Carleton's talent as a poet with wide appeal. "Betsey" was likely a product of pure imagination. "Poor House"—the work that launched him on a new career—came from Carleton's observations at Hillsdale. A public home in the college town

The cobblestone-clad poorhouse made famous by one of Will Carleton's early poems is now a museum maintained by the Hillsdale County Historical Society. Courtesy of Patricia Majher.

provided shelter for the needy. Witnessing firsthand the lack of care for less fortunate relatives by families who abandoned them to the indignity of public support had a lasting impact on the young writer. The latter work tugged on his readers' heartstrings, and they clamored for more.

This second poem launched him on a course that involved retracing his father's emigration from New England. First taking up residence in Boston and then in New York City, where he met his wife, Carleton began to write full-time and published a periodical featuring his works. Within a relatively short time he became seen as the premier American poet of the day. Carleton was far from the pioneer homestead where the first poem about a Native American had been penciled. Yet, in a real way, he had not left Lenawee County. His works carried titles like "Rifts in the Cloud" and "The Song of Home." Poetry collections were published under titles like *Farm Festivals* and *Farm Ballads*. Their popularity—sales of over 100,000 hard-bound volumes during an economic downturn in 1873—confirmed the worth of their themes. Despite living in the nation's center of commerce, Carleton did not focus on urban life or European settings. His writing was about small-town America, county fairs, the simple life in the small village, an honest day's work in the fields and farmyards that resembled nineteenth-century

Lower Michigan. Although he had left the farm in Hudson, he had not left it behind.

During the country's centennial year, Harper & Brothers issued a collection of Carleton poems entitled *Farm Legends*. Though it had been over a decade since his move, the dedication page exhibited Carleton's fondness for an earlier day on a Midwestern homestead: "To the memory of a nobleman," it read, "my farmer father." The preface conveyed a similar sentiment. The author, it said, "has aimed to give expression to the truth, that with every person, even if humble or debased, there may be some good, worth lifting up and saving." Here was a voice that expressed the dignity and value of small-town community.

Carleton's success was not attributable solely to his style of writing. His approach to publishing played an equal role. Each volume of verse numbered between 150 and 180 pages, making them easy reading for most Americans. The books were sold via subscription, using the same mechanism that Mark Twain employed successfully. Pre-selling the book and compensating sales agents for their efforts created a ready market and an aggressive, motivated conduit to bring Carleton's voice to many readers. He was an entrepreneur as well as a bard.

While at Hillsdale, Will had made frequent trips into surrounding villages, earning a few dollars on each occasion by reading his poems to gatherings of farmers and small townspeople hungry for any form of entertainment and enlightenment. As his writing matured and he became more successful, Carleton's readings became as important as his publications. In fact, he is regarded as one of the earliest poets to gain fame and fortune by reading from his published works. The volume of invitations and accompanying compensation grew constantly. It is not certain whether book sales or live performances earned him more income—he could brag of typically earning $100 for a night's performance, a princely sum then. The attraction was quite mutual; Carleton would write of how from an early day, especially in rural Michigan, "I always went away in love with my audience."

In 1877, his popularity prompted the honor of an invitation to be principal speaker in the Memorial Day commemoration at the National Cemetery across the Potomac River from Washington, D.C. We know it as Arlington Cemetery today, a hallowed place of reverence and quietude for hundreds of thousands of graves. It was smaller in 1877, though no less revered. That Decoration Day was sunny, the crowd attentive. Carleton unveiled a work with both personal and national poignancy. It may have been his finest moment.

"Converse with the Slain" consisted of 55 verses in a mythical dialogue between Union Civil War slain and those attending their graves. When delivered on that first occasion, and despite the graveyard setting and purpose to venerate the dead, newspaper accounts reported that the audience interrupted the reading several times with applause and concluded with a standing ovation. The opening of the poem conveys a somber mood:

Here where the Nation's domes salute our eye,
And lift their fingers up to freedom's sky,
Here where, by green-flagged hill and flowery glade,
Camps evermore the Nation's dead brigade,
And, though our stars upon the day are tossed,
White, gleaming head-stones tell of what they cost,
And Triumph's guns are decked with Sorrow's strain,
Let us hold converse with the Nation's slain.

True to his upbringing, the poem was nondiscriminatory. The crowd heard Carleton eulogize:

Men of the dark-hued race,
Whose freedom meant—to die—
Who lie with pain-wrought face
Upturned to the peaceful sky,
Whose day of jubilee,
So many years o'erdue,
Came—but only to be
A day of death to you;
The flowers of whose love grew bright,
E'en in Oppression's track.
. . .

Would that these flowers were bright
As your deeds are true and grand!

The lament ended on a dedicatory note:

> And e'er in realms of glory
> Shine bright your starry claims
> Angels have heard your story
> And God knows all your names.

Carleton did not rely merely on imagination to express the pathos of those who had sacrificed so much to save their country. His brother Henry had served in the 18th Michigan Volunteer Infantry Regiment during the Civil War. Captured and imprisoned in Alabama, after release Henry died somewhere en route back to Hudson. His body was never found.

Carleton's fame continued to grow, and the Memorial Day poem found readings across the land on many anniversaries thereafter. A public hungry for such evocative words filled lecture halls to hear him speak. Eventually he published twelve volumes of poetry, all of them best-selling works, and spoke at thousands of events as the main attraction. During the last three decades of the nineteenth century and into the first of the twentieth, no American writer or public speaker eclipsed his popularity.

Still, Carleton's place in the pantheon of American poets was not secure. The *Evening Wisconsin of Milwaukee* reported in 1902 that "Critics are numerous who would undertake to defend the proposition that he is not a poet, but a producer of rather commonplace verse . . . If literature is the truth about human beings and human life, gleaned by observation or intuition, and embodied in language that cannot be misunderstood and that makes a deep impression upon the reader, some of Carleton's work—especially some of his earliest work—takes rank as literature." The article concluded by comparing the Michigander to Dickens: "They address a larger class of readers than can be reached by the greatest of the sons of song, and they help to make the world better than they find it." Despite contemporary popularity, immortality was far from assured.

After his wife's death, Carleton came back to the farm country in which he had grown up, for one last visit. On October 26, 1907, he stepped off the train in Hudson to discover thousands of well-wishers gathered in his honor. They had come from neighboring farms, from Hillsdale, and all the way from Chicago. A Windy City reporter recounted how the guest of honor "had taught them that there was poetry in every aspect of their practical lives and the sedate landscape." From the porch of the old house, Carleton recited from several of his most famous works and admitted that "this spot is very dear, very sacred to me." As he stood on the porch, looking out over the large crowd, he could see beyond the rows of corn gently swaying over the rolling viewscape toward the horizon, where oaks, elms, and sycamores framed the land he loved, and the people he loved and who loved his verse.

Will Carleton died on December 18, 1912, and was buried in Green-Wood Cemetery in Brooklyn, New York. The works of rhyme, the lectures, and their popularity inspired his native State to venerate his name as unofficial "poet laureate." In Public Act 51, signed into law in 1919, the State of Michigan designated October 21st of each year as "Carleton Day" in memory of "Michigan's pioneer poet." On that day, it was "the duty of each teacher of any grade above fifth grade to read, or cause to be read, to his or her pupils at least one of the poems of Will Carleton." In subsequent years, Will Carleton Day achieved the same rank in observance under Michigan law as Veterans Day, Constitution Day, Columbus Day, and the birthdays of Washington, Lincoln, and Teddy Roosevelt.

Carleton's pantheon place, in Michigan at least, appeared solid. In 1976, however, Carleton Day was stricken from the compiled laws. That year, legendary singer-songwriter Johnny Cash "did his bit to mark" the day at an event in Muskegon, dedicating a song to the Michigan poet. Described as a "Carleton fan," he told reporters, "'I'm probably one of the few people who has a complete set of Will Carleton's books. I've got everything he's ever written.'"[1] Perhaps the Michigan Legislature should have asked the "Man in Black" for his views on the poet's standing. *Harper's Weekly*, the famed national periodical that had brought him to the greater public eye, claimed him as one of America's "most popular poets and the one whose writings have been more widely read and appreciated than those of any poet since the days of Whittier and Longfellow."

Hudson is a small hub of transportation spokes that go east to Adrian, west to Hillsdale, north to Jackson and the Irish Hills, and south into Ohio. Today the traveler can see Carleton's name on a memorial highway through the southern tier of Monroe, Lenawee, Hillsdale, and Calhoun Counties, a route that leaves Hillsdale for parts eastward. That road departs the Hillsdale

College campus, curves and dips by swampy marshes and small lakes, passes near cattails and fallen trees overtaken by ponds and groundwater pools, and parallels a railroad bed that at many places is high above grade. Arriving in the town of Hudson, one finds a historic district full of structures that Carleton knew, including the remnant of an arched stone bridge over Bean Creek, where the Lake Shore & Michigan Southern cars would carry Will Carleton to and from Hillsdale College. East of Hudson, near the top of a small rise and close to the road, sits a farmhouse expanded from the original log house. In front of the home is a large stone, as immutable as the rural virtues it commemorates, with an affixed marker reminding the traveler that here was born Michigan's first great poet. Behind the boulder, the fields gently undulate, still fertile and productive after nearly two hundred years of cultivation, until they fold into the line of trees.

Carleton is the name of an incorporated village in Monroe County about ten miles north of Monroe; the name also can be found on an educational institution in Hillsdale. With all of this evidence, it might be expected that the pioneer poet remains a household name. Most Michiganders today, however, would not know the cause of any of these designations. Previous generations did. They knew of a poet from the Michigan prairie who was born in these regions, lived here, wrote here, and left here for a national stage. The name of Will Carleton is no longer embedded in the fabric of today's society. But under that name was created verse that, during a lifetime and for decades later, reminded all Americans of the nobility and enduring strength of life on a Michigan country lane.

Works

Poems (Chicago: Lakeside Publishing & Printing Co., 1871).
Farm Ballads (New York: Harper and Bros., 1873).
Farm Legends (New York: Harper and Bros., 1875).
Young Folks' Centennial Rhymes (New York: Harper and Bros., 1876).
Why Wife and I Quarreled (New York: G.W. Carleton & Co., 1877).
Farm Festivals (New York: Harper and Bros., 1881).
City Ballads (New York: Harper and Bros., 1886).
An Ancient Spell (Chicago: Clark & Maynard, 1887).

City Legends (New York: Harper and Bros., 1889).

City Festivals (New York: Harper and Bros., 1892).

Rhymes of Our Planet (New York: Harper and Bros., 1895).

The Old Infant and Similar Stories (New York: Harper and Bros., 1896).

Songs of Two Centuries (New York: Harper and Bros., 1902).

In Old School Days (New York: Moffat, Yard and Co., 1907).

Drifted In (New York: Moffat, Yard and Co., 1908).

A Thousand Thoughts with Index of Subjects (New York: Every Where Publishing Co., 1908).

A Thousand More Verses (New York: Every Where Publishing Co., 1912).

Sites

Hudson Downtown Historic District, encompassing West Main Street (M-34) between Howard Street on the west and Market Street on the east, extending on the north to Railroad Street and south to Seward Street, Hudson, Michigan

Lakeshore and Michigan Southern Railroad Bean Creek Stone Arch Bridge, North of Main Street, Hudson, Michigan

Will Carleton Poor House (listed on National and State Register of Historic Sites), 180 North Wolcott Street, Hillsdale, Michigan 49242

Will Carleton homestead, 14995 Carleton Road, Hudson, Michigan

James Oliver Curwood

Champion of God's Country

June 12, 1878–August 13, 1927

Born and grew up in Owosso; attended the University of Michigan; worked for *Detroit News-Tribune*

He did his best work in a castle, hurling down thunderbolts of prose. The fact that James Oliver Curwood was a son of, and died in Owosso, Michigan, made him no less a man of international renown. His fiction and political invective reached audiences far beyond the boundaries of his community and state.

Born in Owosso in 1878, Curwood came by his writing skill and love of the outdoors, it was said, because he was distantly related to both Captain Frederick Marryat, an English storyteller of fame in the first half of the nineteenth century, and an "Indian princess." (Neither claim has been substantiated.) He spent a portion of his childhood in Ohio, but his family returned to Owosso when he was thirteen, and he called the community "home" in his adult life. Fascinated by the outdoors from early childhood, he fell in love with the Shiawassee River, a narrow, meandering stream that is part of the Saginaw Bay watershed. Later in life he cited the pollution of the river as a disgrace, and invoked his boyhood playground as one source of his passion and creativity. He hunted small game as a child and teenager, the start of a sportsman's life that would end only a few years before his life did—a change likened to a religious conversion.

A scribbler from his early days, Curwood is said to have authored a 200,000-word novel at age nine. But it wasn't until age eighteen that his first published story appeared in the Owosso newspaper, the *Argus*. It was an early, significant contribution to a massive body of written work.

Curwood never obtained an Owosso high school diploma, but did well enough on an entrance exam to gain admission to the University of Michigan. Campus life couldn't hold him—and perhaps he didn't give it his all. Imagination and restlessness ended his education after two years at the university. He quit to write for the *Detroit News-Tribune*. By the end of his eight-year stint there, he was spinning yarns of adventure in the outdoors that were accepted by magazines with national circulation, such as *Good Housekeeping* and *Outing*.

He had also made the acquaintance of M. V. "Mac" MacInness, a Canadian official stationed in Detroit. Recognizing Curwood's ability to popularize places as well as stories, MacInness urged the Canadian government to turn the author's writing to advantage. After Curwood spent time in (and wrote about) the wild and vast Canadian North of Hudson Bay and beyond, the Canadian government paid him to visit the west and far north of the nation, hoping his writing would induce settlement, trade, and tourism. That wild range became the stage for many of his books. Curwood used a term for it, "God's Country," in the title of three novels. The phrase came to represent his belief in the power and beauty of the natural world.

Stories and sketches didn't allow space for all that Curwood wanted to tell. In 1907 he left the Detroit newspaper and published two novels, *The Courage of Captain Plum* and *The Wolf Hunters*, the following year. He would produce thirty-three books.

Curwood's works typically featured romantic heroes and heroines, but the most important character was wild nature. It was drawn directly from the original—it is estimated that Curwood spent at least nine months of each year in the woods from 1908 to 1926. He said, "Nature is my religion. And my desire . . . my ambition . . . the great goal I wish to achieve is to take

An aggressive, high-volume conservationist, James Curwood was also a zesty outdoorsman, like the fictional heroes he created in numerous novels featuring adventurers in the remote Canadian north. Photo courtesy of State of Michigan Archives.

my readers with me into the heart of this Nature. I love it, and I feel that they must love it . . . if I can only get the two acquainted."

Since animals, including dogs, were often important characters in his works, and because he wrote of wild, lonely lands, some compared him to Jack London, whose White Fang was a prototype in the literature of animals as characters. Curwood welcomed the comparison.

His works became so popular that he is reputed to have been the first writer to make a million dollars off his craft in a single year, in the 1920s. Contemporary critics were frequently enamored of his writing. In February 1918, the *New York Times Book Review* commented: "Curwood has an invaluable gift of the born narrator—the ability to tell a story and tell it in an interesting and vivid way." The bulletin of the State Library of Michigan in 1920 noted that his fans were "legion."

Curwood writes of the great out-of-doors and portrays the elemental in life, both in nature and in human associations. Weary with their complexes, their income taxes, the din of traffic, and the monotony of daily toil, this great mass of Curwood lovers seek these stories that tell of the simple life unhampered by conventionality, pictured against a backdrop of wilderness . . . Curwood's best books are those in which human beings take the least part.

A characteristic Curwood paragraph can be found in *The Courage of Marge O'Doone*.

The next instant Hauck was at the open door. He did not cross the threshold at once, but stood there for perhaps twenty seconds—his gray, hard face looking in on them with eyes in which there was a cold and sinister glitter. Brokaw, with the fumes of liquor thick in his brain, tried to nod an invitation for him to enter; his head rolled grotesquely and his voice was a croak. David rose slowly to his feet, thrusting back his chair. From contemplating Brokaw's sagging body, Hauck's eyes were leveled at him. And then his lips parted. One would not have called it a smile. It revealed to David a deadly animosity which the man was trying to hide under the disguise of that grin, and he knew that Hauck had discovered that he was not McKenna. Swiftly David shot a glance at Brokaw. The giant's head and shoulders lay on the table, and he made a sudden daring effort to save a little more time for himself.

In 1922 and 1923, using some of the wealth he had reaped from book sales, the author had what is now called the Curwood Castle built on land he owned along the Shiawassee River in the heart of Owosso. The castle was designed loosely in the style of an old French chateau. The stucco exterior contains fieldstones he chose. It contains no eating or sleeping areas. He used the great room to entertain guests, including movie producers, and the largest turret as his writing studio. While in the castle he wrote for hours each morning, crafting one after another novel of gusto.

It was in part that regularity of production that has led critics to be less and less kind to Curwood's writing over the years. He is now described by some as a "pulp writer" of "purple prose" who churned out numerous predictable volumes of idealized characters. Curwood biographer Judith Eldredge observes, "Eventually, though, his fame as a writer faded, his exciting adventure stories forgotten or rejected as old-fashioned and out of date."

James Curwood wrote many of his swashbuckling novels in a castle tailored to his wishes beside his beloved Shiawassee River in Owosso. Courtesy of Michigan State Historic Preservation Office.

Certain features of his writing, though, still have fans. Members of the Royal Canadian Mounted Police were heroes in several of Curwood's books, and many Canadian locales appeared in his works. This setting pleases some Canadians. After picking up Curwood's *Wapi, the Walrus,* Jeffrey Blair Latter wrote, "I was amazed to find an American author had not only set an adventure in boring old Canada, but that he had written about my home in ways that made it sound like the most mysterious, most thrilling place on the planet. Even stranger, as I read about huskies and dog-sleds, trappers and prospectors, I felt an odd sense of familiarity, of coming home—what writers sometimes call 'resonance.'" Several of Curwood's tales featuring animals are still recommended as children's reading.

A devoted hunter, Curwood is said to have eaten a dinner of woolly mammoth while roaming the far north, where his party came upon the ancient animal corpse exposed by the collapse of a cliffside. The author frequently boasted of his hunting exploits. But all at once that changed.

One of his novels, *The Grizzly King*, captured a life-changing moment supposedly drawn from Curwood's own experience while hunting in the Canadian North. Having wounded a bear, the book's protagonist, Langdon, realizes he is trapped on a ledge and at the animal's mercy. The bear chooses not to kill him.

> "You great big god of a bear!" Langdon cried "'You—you monster with a heart bigger than man!' And then he added, under his breath, as if not conscious that he was speaking: 'If I'd cornered you like that I'd have killed you! And you! You cornered me, and let me live!'"

Spared by the enormous creature, Curwood soon became a fervent advocate for restraints on hunting and fishing to preserve wildlife populations for the future. He condemned what he regarded as the politicization of Michigan conservation policy, which he believed had led to the destruction and waste of its timber resources, the pollution of the state's air and waters, and the dramatic decline of its fish and wildlife species. Headlines in Michigan newspapers frequently trumpeted his latest accusations against Michigan governor Alexander Groesbeck and his Department of Conservation in the early 1920s. His roaring diatribes elicited both adulation and bitter condemnation, the latter of which the author dismissed. He wrote one supporter: "Michigan is being cheated out of the birthright of her natural resources because Lansing plays first the game of politics, leaving the welfare of the State and its people a secondary matter."

One of the sources of his reformist energy was the ugly transformation of the river that ran through Owosso. In his autobiography, Curwood wrote: "Such was the Shiawassee of my boyhood—my river—clean and refreshing as it flowed along on all the pride of its ancient lineage. Would to God the greed and selfishness of modern commerce had refrained from polluting it! Verily, nothing is sacred to the overlords of business!" Curwood donated generously to clean up the banks of the river, and bankrolled the stocking of streams with fish, and of preserves with game animals.

Appointed to the state Conservation Commission in early 1927 by Groesbeck's successor, Governor Fred Green, Curwood fought to close hunting seasons on some game and fish. The other members of the commission rebuffed him, some of them considering him a publicity hound with unscientific and politically unrealistic ideas about conservation.

Curwood had spoken often of his diet of copious vegetables and some meat, and his abstinence from alcohol, and had predicted he would live to one hundred because of his clean and robust living. But not long after his final defeat by the commission, he fell ill and died at the age of forty-nine. In his last magazine article, Curwood spoke of the healing powers and spiritual value of the outdoors. He wrote of a friend who had gone numb to life after his wife died. Curwood took him out into the woods and sat with the man, hearing "the musical ripple of a creek," watching a squirrel gnawing on a nut, enjoying a warbler's song, and noting the ambling of a woodchuck. The friend "has brought himself down out of the clouds of man's egoism," Curwood wrote, "and is learning and taking strength from nature, which he now worships as the great 'I am.'"

Curwood's colorful tales of pure women and intrepid men of the Northwest reached the big screen. Filmmakers based at least forty silent and talking films on his plots, including *The Trail Beyond* (1935), which featured John Wayne, and *Back to God's Country* (1953), starring Rock Hudson. The film *Kazan* is typical of his filmed works. Based on Curwood's book of the same name, it features a mighty white dog running wild in the wilderness. After cruel loggers harm him, Kazan learns to trust mankind through the kindness and consideration of a government wildlife expert.

French director Jean-Jacques Annaud chose Curwood's *The Grizzly King* as the inspiration for his 1988 film *The Bear*, which *New York Times* critic Janet Maslin called "a remarkable achievement only on its own terms, which happen to be extremely limited and peculiar." She added that the director had "coaxed from his bear actors performances that are quite a bit better than those of the film's several human players, who get bottom billing." But the *Los Angeles Times* called it "an epic of lost innocence."

Not all literary critics speak harshly of Curwood's legacy. In *The Dictionary of Midwestern Literature* (2001), Donald M. Hassler says Curwood "created classic fiction in the modes of romance adventure and the particularly American version of nature romanticism."

Although largely forgotten in the literary world, Curwood is remembered today in three ways. The writer's castle still stands on the banks of the Shiawassee. Outside it stands a state historical marker that describes him as at one time "the most popular [author] in North America" and "a zealous conservationist." The Owosso-based Curwood Festival, held in early June each year since 1978, brings locals and tourists to visit the studio, participate in a raft race on the Shiawassee, sample arts and crafts, drink and eat enthusiastically, and enjoy a parade. In 2010, the festival included an event paying homage to both Curwood and participants' "childhood wonderment and joy," calling to mind the author's childhood romps along the river and in his imagination. The theme for the 33rd festival was "Fantasy and Fiction." Another Curwood legacy is the slowly healing Shiawassee River, where environmental laws have reduced sewage and industrial pollution. Still, in recent years, river cleanup volunteers have retrieved dozens of scrap tires, appliances, and other discards from its banks and waters.

Far to the north, in one of the most remote parts of the state in Michigan's Upper Peninsula, not far from where Curwood once owned a cabin, stands the 1,980-foot Mount Curwood. For many years, maps advertised it as the highest point in Michigan, but late in the twentieth century a new measurement gave that honor to nearby 1,981-foot Mount Arvon. Larger than life during his career, Curwood has often been eclipsed in the decades since his death.

Works

The Courage of Captain Plum (New York: Bobbs-Merrill, 1908; Grosset & Dunlap, 1912).

The Wolf Hunters: A Tale of Adventure in the Outdoors (New York: Bobbs-Merrill, 1908).

The Great Lakes: The Vessels That Plough Them, Their Owners, Their Sailors and Their Cargoes, Together with a Brief History of Our Inland Seas (New York: G.P. Putnam's Sons, Knickerbocker Press, 1909).

The Gold Hunters: A Story of Life and Adventure in the Hudson Bay Wilds (New York: McKinlay, Stone and Mackenzie, 1909).

The Danger Trail (New York: Grosset and Dunlap, 1910).

The Honor of the Big Snows (New York: Bobbs-Merrill, 1911).

Steele of the Royal Mounted: A Story of the Great Canadian Northwest (New York: A.L Burt Co., 1911).

The Flower of the North: A Modern Romance (New York and London: Harper and
   Bros., 1912).

Isobel: A Romance of the Northern Trail (New York and London: Harper and
   Bros., 1913).

Kazan (New York: Grosset and Dunlap, 1914).

God's Country—and the Woman (New York: A.L. Burt Co., 1915).

The Grizzly King (New York: Doubleday, Page and Co., 1915).

The Hunted Woman: A Romance of the Wild (New York: Grosset and Dunlap, 1916).

Baree, Son of Kazan (New York: Grosset and Dunlap, 1917).

The Courage of Marge O'Doone (New York: Grosset and Dunlap, 1918, 1920).

Nomads of the North (New York: Grosset and Dunlap, 1919).

The River's End (New York: McKinlay, Stone and Mackenzie, 1919).

Back to God's Country and Other Stories (New York: Grosset and Dunlap, 1920).

The Valley of Silent Men: A Story of the Three River Country (New York:
   Cosmopolitan Book Corp., 1920).

God's Country—The Trail to Happiness (New York: McKinlay, Stone and
   Mackenzie, 1921).

The Golden Snare (New York: Grosset and Dunlap, 1921).

The Flaming Forest: A Novel of the Canadian Northwest (New York: Cosmopolitan
   Book Corp., 1921).

The Country Beyond: A Romance of the Wilderness (New York: Grosset and
   Dunlap, 1922).

The River's End: A New Story of God's Country (New York: Grosset and
   Dunlap, 1922).

The Alaskan (New York: Cosmopolitan Book Corp., 1923).

A Gentleman of Courage: A Novel of the Wilderness (New York: Cosmopolitan
   Book Corp., 1924).

The Ancient Highway: A Novel of High Hearts and Open Woods (New York:
   Cosmopolitan Book Corp., 1925).

Swift Lightning: A Story of Wildlife Adventure in the Frozen North (New York:
   Grosset and Dunlap, 1926).

The Black Hunter: A Novel of Old Quebec (New York: Grosset and Dunlap, 1926).

The Plains of Abraham (New York: Doubleday, Doran and Co., 1928).

The Crippled Lady of Peribonka (New York: Doubleday, Doran and Co., 1929).

Green Timber (New York: Grosset and Dunlap, 1930).

Son of the Forests: An Autobiography (New York: Doubleday, Doran and Co., 1930).

Falkner of the Inland Seas (New York: Grosset and Dunlap, 1931).

The Glory of Living: The Autobiography of an Adventurous Boy Who Grew into a Writer and a Lover of Life (Mattituck, NY: Aeonian Press, 1983).

The Bear: A Novel (New York: Newmarket Press, 1989).

Sites

· ·

Curwood Castle, 224 Curwood Castle Drive, Owosso, Michigan 48867

Oak Hill Cemetery, 1101 S. Washington, Owosso, Michigan: Curwood Grave

Curwood Festival, Owosso, Michigan, each June

Marguerite de Angeli
Children Don't Forget

March 14, 1889–June 16, 1987
Born in and grew up in Lapeer; lived in Detroit

. . . .

There is a garden in every childhood, an enchanted place where colors are brighter, the air softer, and the morning more fragrant than ever again.—ELIZABETH LAWRENCE

In 1889 Lapeer, Michigan, was not much different from many other small Midwestern towns. But the combination of a family's nurturing and a girl's temperament and budding talent fostered one of America's most successful authors of children's books.

Marguerite de Angeli was born that year in a house at the intersection of Main and Oregon Streets. Her maternal and paternal families, the Tattles and the Loffts, were engaged in business related to the area's original industries, lumbering and farming. The lure of, first, the primeval timber and, later, when the trees were cleared, family farming attracted early generations of Lapeer residents. The settled town soon teemed with business and community activity. The Lofft family was known for its engagement in the local Methodist church, and William Lofft, Marguerite's grandfather, was a blacksmith. The Tuttles were a prosperous family with a lumber business.

In the years after her birth on Main on March 14, 1889, Marguerite Lofft experienced Lapeer as "lovely and like a park." Trees remaining from the original forest dotted yards. Home life was a park, too, she always thought. Her father, Shad Lofft, and mother, Ruby, sheltered Marguerite and her five siblings from life's blows. One of the blows was the undependable income of Shad's photography work, which forced almost annual moving into new quarters.

Despite being uprooted multiple times, Marguerite was secure in the constancy of her family. Remembering her father's light baritone voice accompanied by her mother's piano playing, she said, "I think I have always had a need for reassurance, and this part of our family life seemed to provide it, along with his Sunday morning habit of smoking a cigar, which sent a fragrant wreath about his head." But she noted she missed him on his increasingly frequent journeys out of Lapeer in search of income.

The story goes that when only two, Marguerite began to interest herself in the crayons her father used to hand-tint his photographs. Her child's curiosity led her to begin drawing with the chalks. Within two or three years, books on her father's shelves began to fascinate her. She laid some of them, too big to hold, on the floor and studied them. Soon she was dreaming of making books of her own. And dreaming "how I could put down in words the sheer joy in living which thrilled me to bursting," and drawing village scenes of sunlight, trees, and children.

As Marguerite became a teenager, the family moved from Lapeer to Philadelphia, where her father found work at the Eastman Kodak Company. Although she thrived on the opportunities offered by life in a major city, the comfort and enchantment of Lapeer never left her.

Marguerite developed another artistic talent in Philadelphia, taking voice lessons, joining church choirs as a paid vocalist, and meeting her husband-to-be John Dailey de Angeli, first violin in the Philadelphia Orchestra. In love with the "born salesman" Dai, she faced a choice between joining the cast of Oscar Hammerstein's opera company for an opera tour, or accepting Dai's wedding proposal. She chose family life, marrying de Angeli in Toronto in 1910. The marriage would last fifty-nine years.

The young couple moved, as her own family had done, almost constantly at first, following Dai's work establishing dealerships for Edison phonographs.

Marguerite de Angeli in her childhood, which she remembered fondly for family intimacy and small-town community. Her grandfather's attic, where she played as a child, was the setting for "Ted and Nina Have a Happy Rainy Day." Lapeer also served as the backdrop for her book "Copper-Toed Boots." Courtesy of Lapeer District Library.

They moved through western Canada, to Minneapolis, and then to Detroit, where Dai worked for the J.L. Hudson Company. Finally, Marguerite prevailed upon her husband to return east, settling in Collingswood, New Jersey. Along the way she bore five children, one of whom, Ruby Catherine, died in infancy.

At the age of thirty-two, Marguerite got help from a neighbor, Maurice Bower, an illustrator for Hearst publications, as a tutor. Marguerite's drawings began appearing in publications like *The Country Gentleman* and *The American Girl*. For three years her work was published each month. She balanced career with home, dealing at one point with her one-year-old son Ted's love of climbing out his crib, and onto her drawing table, by standing in the playpen herself with her easel, and allowing her son free run of the room. Much later she also credited her children with helping her illustrate lifelike children. "When I had the children, I found how to draw children and I studied anatomy when I bathed them. Even their bones and how they connected and so forth."

"I had wanted to write almost as much as I could draw, and felt that I could easily write a story for a six-year-old," Marguerite wrote in her autobiography. Helen Ferris of the Junior Literary Guild asked her to write a children's book. Fifteen years after beginning her career as an illustrator, Marguerite became a published author. Entitled *Ted and Nina Go to the Grocery Store*, using the names of two of her children, the book contains a simple tale, which she illustrated herself, of a journey steeped in nostalgia for a simpler time. It begins:

Ted and Nina are two little children just like you.

Ted is four years old. Ted wears a striped jersey. He goes to kindergarten.

Nina is six years old. Nina wears a plaid skirt. She goes to school. Tippy, the little
dog, is just a puppy.

At Mr. Jones's grocery store, the two children meet a "very pleasant" grocer and are riveted at the sight of vibrant fruits and vegetables; meat, fish, and oysters; cheese, lard, and cookies. Toting home a heavy basket of items from a list provided by their mother, they are greeted by Tippy at the gate— and Mother at the door. One of the first books designed for children to read to themselves, *Ted and Nina* was successfully created to appeal to the young eye with vivid illustrations whose images were painted on separate glass plates and then overlaid to show striking color.

This successful title was followed by *Ted and Nina Have a Happy Rainy Day*. Later came *A Summer Day with Ted and Nina*. When the three stories appeared in one book, Marguerite dedicated them to the real Ted and Nina, who, "though seven years apart, were very close to each other, and still are. Now each has children of his own."

The author began turning out children's volumes regularly, including *Henner's Lydia*, about the life of an Amish family in the Pennsylvania Dutch country, which she researched by charming a real family into showing her their lifeways. Another book, *Petite Suzanne*, was based on research conducted with a week-long stay with a French Canadian family in the Gaspé Peninsula.

Her native Michigan village was the scene and subject of 1938's *Copper-Toed Boots*. Dedicated to her father, Shad, and his boyhood friend Ash, the book imaginatively describes Shad's own childhood in the 1870s as the son of a blacksmith. A small-town evening's mood is characterized by "the cool green of the sky," the pure white of houses against the dark trees and bushes, and the scent of lilies of the valley in a neighbor's garden. Young adventurers, Shad and Ash in one scene race to the woods—the nearest woods, that is, because Shad's father had warned him away from the second, more distant woods with their giant white pines, tamaracks, dark spruce trees, swampy ground, pine snakes, rattlesnakes, and even a black bear. "But Shad didn't care; there was lots of fun in the first woods." Wanting to make arrows, the boys come upon an arrowhead left by Native Americans and crafted from local stones. The author notes that the name "Lapeer" translates from French as "a stone."

Marguerite fashioned more than quaint, simple tales of childhood. Two of her children's books dared to challenge societal norms. Published in 1946, *Bright April* takes on racial prejudice. Set in Philadelphia, it shows how children are able to gain understanding and tolerance on their own. April is an African American girl whose sunny personality dissolves prejudice on her tenth birthday. At the end of the book, April comforts a white girl during a storm by climbing into bed with her, a scene her editor initially advised against.

The inspiration for the book was a conversation with the de Angeli's housekeeper, Medora, whose son (in Nina's class) was unaccompanied by any classmate in the high school graduation procession. But Nina took care of that by walking with him. Saying *Bright April* might have been the first children's book featuring children of different races, de Angeli told a reporter, "I tried to emphasize likenesses rather than differences."[1]

Doubleday, the publisher, delayed releasing the book by six years because of the subject matter. And there is even a vestige of archaic racial attitudes in the index of Marguerite's autobiography, where *Bright April* is characterized in parentheses as "Negro book." Marguerite's son Arthur, who encouraged her to write the book, warned her she might be called a communist "or some other unpleasant name." But the author was undeterred. Today, *Bright April* is a landmark in children's book publishing.

A 1949 book, *The Door in the Wall*, fought prejudice against those with physical disabilities. The thirteenth-century young English hero, Robin, struggles with lameness. A monk named Brother Luke helps guide him along the path to recognizing his own worth, telling Robin, "It is better to have crooked legs than a crooked spirit." Robin's personal heroism affirms his dignity and confirms the monk's counsel: "Thou hast only to follow the wall far enough and there will be a door in it."

This time, Marguerite's creative source was a neighbor at their summer cottage, Harmon Robinson. Largely bedridden for three years beginning at the age of ten, "Harm" had to crawl on his hands and knees or use crutches. Unfazed, he developed his musical talent and was a friend of many. Marguerite remembered, "He ignored his disability as far as possible, but gave in to it when it seemed necessary. I think he was always in some pain and he often slept on a small divan, with his feet on one armrest and his head on the other. We admired and loved him."

Reviewers were charmed and enthusiastic. The *New York Times* called it "an enthralling and inspiring tale of triumph over handicap. Unusually beautiful illustrations, full of authentic detail, combine with the text to make life in England during the Middle Ages come alive." The *New Yorker* magazine called it "a poignant story, full of action, and a strongly painted canvas of the times as well."

The Door in the Wall astonished its author by winning the iconic 1950 Newbery Award for children's books. Typically crediting her editor Peggy Lesser and her friend "Harm," she spoke in her acceptance speech generally of her belief that people have few basic differences and that "it is only in the non-essentials that we differ; what we have for breakfast, and how we greet our parents, or a different way of expressing the same homely truths, those bits of wisdom that have grown out of ages of experience."

Other awards followed. *Black Fox of Lorne*, aimed at older children, was a Newbery Honor Book in 1957. The story occurs in the tenth century and features Viking twins shipwrecked on the Scottish coast. *Yonie Wondernose* and the *Book of Nursery and Mother Goose Rhymes* were Caldecott Honor Books in 1945 and 1955, respectively. For the latter, the best selling of her books, Marguerite selected and illustrated 376 rhymes.

Award-winning children's author Marguerite de Angeli returned occasionally in later life to read and tell children about her books at the Lapeer library named in her honor. Courtesy of Lapeer District Library.

She frequently responded to invitations from her hometown. In 1941, 1950, and 1963 she returned to Lapeer. On the 1963 trip, a *Lapeer County Press* reporter who interviewed Marguerite observed that the author had long "belonged to Philadelphia. But her heart, which never grew old, belongs to Lapeer." On another visit, her hosts took her to see the old house on Main Street where she had lived, and on still another, the owners of her Grandfather Tuttle's expansive house led her up to the attic that had been her playground in childhood, and had been the imaginary setting of *Ted and Nina Have a Happy Rainy Day.* The countryside encircling Lapeer charmed her on drives.

Marguerite continued publishing original work until her late eighties, and was not forgotten by the children of her home community at White Junior High School. They researched her works and asked Governor William G. Milliken to proclaim March 14, 1979—Marguerite's ninetieth birthday—as

"Marguerite de Angeli Day in Michigan." Although generally unwilling to declare days for individuals, the governor wrote the class that "your gesture was inspiring enough to warrant a rare exception." Marguerite, the proclamation said, was "an inspiration to young writers and will forever be fondly regarded by the people of Lapeer and the State of Michigan."

Marguerite, thrilled, thanked the class in a letter, unable to attend her own day in Michigan because of a special day sponsored by the Free Library of Philadelphia, a city that claimed her as its own. Named a Distinguished Daughter of Pennsylvania, Marguerite won recognition from the governor of that state and from the mayor of Philadelphia, as well as fan mail and flowers on her ninetieth birthday. She was able to visit her Lapeer junior high school admirers in May of the same year. She reminisced about the Lapeer of her youth—Uncle Denny's jewelry store, her father's photograph gallery, Uncle Steve Lockwood's general store.

When Lapeer's public library was renamed in her honor in 1981, Marguerite said, "It means a great deal to me that I am loved in Lapeer." In 1984, Marguerite was inducted into the Michigan Women's Hall of Fame.

Born in a small Michigan village that might have been bounded by provincial beliefs, Marguerite de Angeli invoked her gentle childhood and comfort there to imagine with compassion how it might be to live under the shadow of prejudice. She taught a generation of young people to look behind the outer shell of humanity to see the person inside. In so doing, she left behind even more than the Marguerite de Angeli Library and collection in her native Lapeer.

Works

. . . .

Ted and Nina Go to the Grocery Store (Garden City, NY: Doubleday, Doran and Co., 1935).

Ted and Nina Have a Happy Rainy Day (Garden City, NY: Doubleday, Doran and Co., 1936).

Henner's Lydia (Garden City, NY: Doubleday, Doran and Co., 1936).

Petite Suzanne (Garden City, NY: Doubleday, Doran and Co., 1937).

Copper-Toed Boots (Garden, NY: Doubleday, Doran and Co., 1938).

Skippack School: Being the Story of Eli Shrawder and of One Christopher Dock, Schoolmaster About the Year 1750 (Garden City, NY: Doubleday, Doran and Co., 1939).

A Summer Day with Ted and Nina (Garden City, NY: Doubleday, Doran and Co., 1940).

Thee, Hannah! (Garden City, NY: Doubleday, Doran and Co., 1940).

Elin's Amerika (Garden City, NY: Doubleday, Doran and Co., 1941).

Up the Hill (Garden City, NY: Doubleday, Doran and Co., 1942).

Yonie Wondernose (Garden City, NY: Doubleday, Doran and Co., 1944).

Turkey for Christmas (Philadelphia: Westminster Press, 1944).

Bright April (Garden City, NY: Junior Literary Guild, Doubleday and Co., 1946).

Jared's Island (Garden City, NY: Junior Literary Guild, Doubleday and Co., 1947).

The Door in the Wall (Garden City, NY: Doubleday and Co., 1949).

Just Like David (Garden City, NY: Junior Literary Guild: Doubleday and Co., 1951).

Book of Nursery and Mother Goose Rhymes (Garden City, NY: Doubleday and Co., 1954).

Black Fox of Lorne (Garden City, NY: Doubleday and Co., 1956).

A Pocket Full of Posies: A Merry Mother Goose (Garden City, NY: Doubleday and Co., 1961).

The Goose Girl: A New Translation (Garden City, NY: Doubleday and Co., 1964).

Turkey for Christmas (with Arthur de Angeli) (Philadelphia: Westminster Press, 1965).

The Empty Barn (Philadelphia: Westminster Press, 1966).

Butter at the Old Price: The Autobiography of Marguerite de Angeli (Garden City, NY: Doubleday and Co., 1971).

Fiddlestrings (Garden City, NY: Doubleday and Co., 1974).

The Lion in the Box (Garden City, NY: Doubleday and Co., 1975).

Whistle for the Crossing (Garden City, NY: Doubleday and Co., 1977).

Friendship and Other Poems (Garden City, NY: Doubleday and Co., 1981).

Sites

· ·

Marguerite de Angeli Library, 921 West Nepessing Street, Lapeer, Michigan 48446

Tuttle House, 610 N. Main Street, Lapeer, Michigan: the site celebrated by
Marguerite de Angeli in her 1936 book *Ted and Nina Have a Happy Rainy Day*.

Women's Hall of Fame, 213 W. Main Street, Lansing, Michigan 48933.

Holling Clancy Holling

Beyond Four Corners

August 2, 1900–September 7, 1973
Born and lived in Henrietta Township; graduate of Leslie High School; visitor to Au Sable

Unlike the devil, the glacier that scoured out the Great Lakes didn't first go down to Georgia, only to Tennessee. This massive mountain of frozen water once buried Michigan and, returning homeward after a 10,000-year southern stay, left in its wake five major interlocked freshwater lakes. Viewed from the stratosphere, the outlines of the outstretched Lower Peninsula and its northern neighbor are unmistakable. Other states of the Union are not so blessed. Their boundaries are legal fictions, created from surveyors' transits and consisting of straight lines designed by political bargains. Michigan, on the other hand, owes its contours to forces much purer.

Almost equidistant in the southern peninsula from two of those great lakes, Erie and Michigan, a point exists. Imaginary boundaries intersect here: one, a meridian, slices the Lower Peninsula into two halves; the other, mirroring the equator, forms a base line. Where these lines cross once served as the key reference point for surveyors to devise Michigan's township lines. Today, the site is a unique historic state park—inaccessible to the public, completely surrounded by wood lots and private lands.

Holling Clancy Holling drew upon the natural world of his youth in mid-Michigan to create inspiring picture books for young people. As his rural grave marker proclaims, he lives on in those works. Courtesy of the Leslie Area Historical Society Museum.

Less than a mile from here, as two centuries intersected, Holling Allison Clancy was born on August 2, 1900, the son of Bennett Allison Clancy and Lulah Holling. The house in which he was born, still standing, is multi-gabled, a complexity belying its rural setting. The boy was awarded his mother's maiden name as a legacy of her pioneer stock and to prolong it one more generation, for she was the last of her line. From this landlocked birthplace, from this rural boyhood, would emerge an imagination that fashioned magnificent journeys through American history and geography, a creativity that found its fulfillment on the written and illustrated page.

Henrietta Township, the Hollings' neighborhood, was equal parts farm-land and forest. North of Jackson and south of Lansing, the area is thoroughly rural; there are just a few hamlets, carrying names like Fitchburg and Munith. Today, not far away, the Phyllis Haehnle Memorial Audubon Sanctuary provides a wildlife refuge for descendants of the fauna that fascinated the boy Holling in the meadows around his home. He grew up roaming these woods, reading nature books his father (a principal and school superintendent) and mother would bring home. His interests early on were fixed on animals, Indians, and camping. Like many children, Holling loved to draw at an early age; unlike most, at three years old he was fashioning images of animals worthy of an artist far beyond his age. It became obvious that his life would be devoted to something creative, and he settled on the goal of creating children's books.

Achieving this dream required specialized schooling. After graduating from Leslie High School, Holling studied at the Art Institute of Chicago. Not only did he receive a diploma, it was here where he made an important artistic decision: he began using his first name as a signature, making it his surname. It was also where he met Lucille Webster, who would become his wife. After a stint in New Mexico, he went back to Chicago to work at the Field Museum in the taxidermy department, returning to his childhood fascination with animals. After their 1925 marriage, the couple were invited to serve as art instructors on a tour sponsored by New York University. The maiden University World Cruise lasted over seven months, visited thirty-five countries, educated some four hundred students, and employed fifty members of an international faculty that included the Universities of Turin, Washington, Texas, Vienna, and Michigan. Among these scholars was the young Holling, who illustrated the commemorative book after the voyage was over.

The NYU cruise wasn't his first shipboard experience; he had worked on a Great Lakes ore freighter on a couple of occasions, where he fitted out his bunk with a light that enabled reading and sketching during the night. Before eventually settling down in California, where they became designers and illustrators of books by others, the couple traveled through North America, clocking more than 100,000 miles in their auto and trailer. Over the next decade, Holling incorporated these travel experiences as he worked on various children's books, wrote a few, did the pictures for many others . . . but still had in mind realizing a bigger dream.

In 1941, he succeeded. Houghton Mifflin—publisher of school textbooks— came out with a different kind of picture book, uniquely designed by the man from Henrietta Township. It did not tell fairy tales; it did not focus on anthropomorphic characters. It did not describe an implausible story that necessitated the suspension of disbelief; nor were the illustrations comical or juvenile. Rather, the tale told and pictured inside this children's volume challenged its reader far beyond what was typical. For one thing, the pictures were treated differently than in nearly any other such book: the right-hand page was filled with a beautiful watercolor, a work of art that advanced the story line, while the left-hand page held the text—but not conventionally so, for in the margins, top, left, or bottom, were found small maps and pictures, miniature diagrams and other instructional images, which delved deeply into details of the story. These marginalia were intricate. Nothing had been done like this before.

Paddle-to-the-Sea told the account of a carved man-in-canoe launched in Nipigon, Ontario, by a young resident of the Lake Helen Indian Reserve. The little craft made its way down into Lake Superior thanks to the spring melt, journeying to the western edge of the big lake and then along the southern shore to the St. Mary's River. Traversing through the Soo Canal, protagonist Paddle next made the entire length of Lake Michigan, only to turn around for a trip back through the Straits of Mackinac into Lake Huron. Down the St. Clair River, down past Detroit, out across Lake Erie and over Niagara Falls, ultimately Paddle journeyed into the Atlantic where . . . well, the ending should be reserved for the reader. It is an epic tale, the genesis of which is a simple action of a boy trusting to great waters to carry a toy canoe far away to sea. *Paddle* opened up the imagination of each young person who would crack open the book, as many did.

No preposterous story, the tale derived from a canoe trip Holling and a friend (the father of J. H. Chapman, named on the dedication page) started from Chicago's Navy Pier, following the Lake Michigan shoreline and concluding on the shore of the Upper Peninsula. Reminiscent of the sculpture fountain on the grounds of the Art Institute of Chicago, a margin note in the book described how "the Great Lakes are like bowls on a hillside," one spilling into the next until the last flows down the length of a mighty river and into one of Earth's two great oceans. The image of five interconnected bowls suggests a larger picture: Michigan's 11,000 smaller lakes; multitudes of ponds; networks of rivers, streams, creeks, and drains, with their delicate wetlands, fens, and bogs—all link into the five giant freshwater seas as well. It was *Moby Dick* that had recounted "their interflowing aggregate,

A tributary of the Grand River near Hollings Corners in the center of Michigan, where the writer/illustrator spent an idyllic youth. Photo by Jack Dempsey.

those grand fresh-water seas of ours," their "oceanlike expansiveness" and "round archipelagoes of romantic isles." Water—fresh water, water from heaven, spring-fed water—has long formed an integral part of Michigan's identity. Holling's story could not have memorialized his home state more appropriately.

Seventy years later, the book has never been out of print and remains available from its original publisher. Such a feat is rare for a book for young people. Unlike Melville's great classic, *Paddle* embodied the greatest respect for those who were here before the Europeans arrived. The *New York Times* said it exhibited freshness, originality, and imagination. The *New York Herald Tribune* used even stronger terms, like "striking" and "compelling," carrying "a cargo of information."

Holling's objective in these works is found in the introduction to a later work, *Seabird*: "A writer of books for young people is quite aware that they may open new vistas for fresh and eager minds. If this story charts a course into related stories—sparkling seas now held unknown between other book covers—then Seabird will have accomplished part of her mission." It was from Holling's childhood days in Michigan, from his experience on the Great Lakes, that much in these books arose: "It was 'a wooden chip in Niagara's foam showed me how Paddle did it.'" Craftsmanship shone through in the images found in these books, for he did not merely use imagination to figure what they looked like: "The models of Paddle, Tree, and Seabird I made now watch me while I work. There are times when it is easy for me to believe they might actually have experienced their adventures." The young reader would have no doubt of this truth.

Minn of the Mississippi, another in the line, was dedicated to his niece, Linda Lu Mahoney. "Her mother Gwendalin once watched my peculiar scribblings," he wrote in its dedication. Edward, her father, had brought a crock of turtles from the Au Sable River for her enjoyment. The book's Acknowledgment revealed, regarding the animal hero, a turtle—"Hadn't I caught bushels of them in Grandfather's woodlot pond? Yet that was long ago. How long I didn't realize until, on a visit to Michigan, this book was begun. Much had been forgotten, and much I really had never known." Michigan's great rivers, the one bearing "Grand" as its name in his boyhood neighborhood, and the famed Au Sable up north, formed his inspiration.

Minn is also of interest for another reason besides its subtle Michigan influence. At the top of page 52, on the left-hand side where one would typically find a small Holling sidebar, is a rather curious map. It portrays the Mississippi River from Galena, Illinois, down to Grafton where the Illinois River joins in; it follows the Illinois up to Chicago and Lake Michigan. Then, extraneously, it shows the west coast of Michigan, the cities of St. Joseph and Benton Harbor and South Haven, and the St. Joseph River as it winds through Niles down to South Bend and back into Michigan to Hillsdale. It depicts part of the Kalamazoo River from that city east to Battle Creek. Of all things, the map then portrays the Grand River back towards its source as it flows out of Leslie, Rives, and Jackson. In the crease of the book is the Huron River, with some towns listed. Between these last two named rivers, neither having any connection to the story line about the Father of American Rivers—almost lost if one does not carefully read each detail—are two names: "Munith," and "Henrietta."

Holling obviously could not resist including a margin map showing his readers—young minds that he greatly respected—his own backyard as a boy, where streams and rivers originated and began to course their way into the lake that Chicago bordered on. Indeed, a number of maps in these five books show parts of Michigan never strictly necessary for anything in the story.

The Caldecott Medal has been awarded every year since 1938 to the artist of the most distinguished American children's picture book. In its fifth year, the award went to Robert McCloskey for the immortal *Make Way for Ducklings*. Three "Honor Books" were named, runners-up that deserved special commendation above all other American children's picture books published that year. *Paddle* was one of the three. A similar award, the Newbery Medal, has been given annually since 1922 to the most distinguished American children's book—here, winners need contain no illustrations. In 1949, Holling's *Seabird* was an Honor Book; in 1952, his *Minn of the Mississippi* achieved the same high rank. Not many authors and illustrators have been so noted. Grand Rapids–born Chris Van Allsburg is one; Flint's Christopher Paul Curtis is another. Holling was first.

Holling's talent carried him to the Walt Disney Studios for work during the 1940s. Disney brought him back years later as a consultant on several films, and in the design for the California theme park. One of Disney's classic animated films, *Bambi*, benefited from Holling's illustrations. According to the company's official records, the production strove for realism in making a motion picture that properly represented its animal characters. Its artists listened to lectures from animal experts, made trips to the Los Angeles Zoo, watched nature footage, and studied real subjects. Holling's background perfectly suited him to be a member of the team that created this immortal children's movie. His talent also paved the way for illustrating a dozen Quaker Oats cereal-box covers; each featured a famed explorer and his discovery in an "American Frontiers" series.

For someone so gifted, the veteran of such amazing experiences that could inspire such work, one might expect a trove of biographical information to exist and much artistic appreciation to be written. But one must search high and low for material and evaluations. A commentator who found Holling worthy of study practically pleaded for someone to do a full-length treatment. In the reviews that are still in print is found these kinds of judgments: "A writer with the consummate gift of storytelling and the ability to teach through sharing remarkable bits and pieces of information"; a producer of "singular books which offer blendings of rare elements" and "a unique vision of the country"; a "tremendously original and arresting story"; a "vibrant text and imagery." Holling deserves more.

On September 7, 1973, his pen was forever retired when Holling Clancy Holling passed away in California. There remained, however, one final journey. Press accounts cited Holling Corners, Michigan, as his birthplace. Perhaps the name derived from a place like Grover's Corners in *Our Town*. As in so much of his work, however, the place was much more one of imagination than map. The only logical place that Holling Corners might have existed was at the corner of West Territorial Road and Meridian Road in Henrietta Township, a location once owned by two Holling forebears, consisting of nearly 60 acres with the original homestead on the northeast corner, and 75 acres to the west. Holling's remains were brought back to a little country cemetery at the junction of Lowden and Nims Roads, north of (appropriately named) Pleasant Lake in the township. His grave was placed next to those of his parents and brother.

The fields surrounding Nims Cemetery are plowed up in spring. The country lanes are bordered by mature trees, and the one-acre burial ground is as much a part of the landscape as any living thing. The site is bucolic; the grounds start on Nims Road and gently rise toward the west, cresting on a small hill. It is here where, on the western slope, Holling's marker can be found, facing east toward the rising sun. It bears an image of an open book, within which is his pen name in cursive form. The stone has no dates, but rather this apt statement: "Part of Him Lives on in His Books."

Works

New Mexico Made Easy, with Words of Modern Syllables (Chicago: Rockwell F. Clancy Co., 1923).
Sun & Smoke: Verse and Woodcuts of New Mexico (self-published, 1923).
Little Big Bye-and-Bye (Chicago: P.F. Volland, 1926).
Rum-Tum-Tummy (New York: Gordon Volland and Buzza Co., 1927).

Roll Away Twins (Chicago: P.F. Volland, 1927).

The Rollaway Twins (Minneapolis: Buzza Co., Gordon Volland Publication, 1928).

Claws of the Thunderbird: A Tale of Three Lost Indians (Chicago: P.F. Volland, 1928).

Rocky Billy: The Story of the Bounding Career of a Rocky Mountain Goat (New York: Macmillan, 1928).

Choo-Me-Shoo, the Eskimo (New York: Buzza Volland Co., 1928).

The Hidden Treasure (New York: Platt & Munk, 1929).

The Book of Indians (New York: Platt & Munk, 1935).

The Book of Cowboys (New York: Platt & Munk, 1936).

Little Buffalo Boy (Garden City, NY: Garden City Publishing Co., 1939).

Paddle-to-the-Sea (Boston: Houghton Mifflin, 1941).

Tree in the Trail (Boston: Houghton Mifflin, 1942).

Seabird (Boston: Houghton Mifflin, 1948).

Minn of the Mississippi (Boston: Houghton Mifflin, 1951).

Pagoo (Boston: Houghton Mifflin, 1957).

Sites

Hollings Corners, intersection of West Territorial Road and Meridian Road in Henrietta Township, Michigan

Meridian-Baseline Historic State Park, in an area of Jackson County (Michigan) bounded by Meridian Road on the east, Olds Road on the north, Cooper Road on the west, and East Territorial Road on the south

Nims Cemetery, corner of Nims Road and Lowden Road, Pleasant Lake, Michigan (Jackson County)

Theodore Huebner Roethke

The Purity of Despair

May 25, 1908–August 1, 1963

Born and raised in Saginaw; graduate of the University of Michigan; instructor at Michigan State University

When tragedies darken early childhood, they often shape a lasting prelingual worldview of life as frighteningly unsafe. But it can be just as painful to suffer enormous losses in later childhood and adolescence, when language provides the precise vocabulary to enumerate them.

One of the most celebrated of America's twentieth-century poets, Theodore Huebner Roethke remembered the first fifteen years of life in Saginaw after his May 25, 1908, birth as a generally untroubled time. He grew up at 1805 Gratiot, today a museum owned and operated by the Friends of Theodore Roethke Foundation and fronted by a commemorative state historical marker.

Working in his family's renowned greenhouses—the largest in the state at 250,000 square feet before their sale in 1922—Roethke also developed an appreciation for less manicured nature in a 22-acre open space behind the Roethke home. Theodore's cousin said the spot was called simply "The Field"—a name that survives in his final book, *The Far Field*. She said the two played there as children among lilacs and poplars.

Roethke as a teacher at the University of Washington, where he spent his final years and left an indelible memory in the minds of his students. Courtesy of University of Washington Libraries, Special Collections, UW 20147z.

There was another, even wilder place west of town owned by his father and uncle. Originally a land of enormous pine trees and vast marshes, the Saginaw Valley had been thoroughly logged in the second half of the nineteenth century, but Roethke long remembered the beauty of the recovering woods and wetlands in the nature preserve.

"I had several worlds to live in, which I felt were mine," he said in 1953. "One favorite place was a swampy corner of the game sanctuary where herons always nested." He remembered the land as "a wild area of cutover second-growth timber."

The influence of nature on Roethke was lifelong. "I have a genuine love of nature. It is not the least bit affected but an integral and powerful part of my life . . . Ever since I could walk, I have spent as much time as I could in the open," he wrote.

The greenhouses, too, would persist in his memory. His 1948 collection *The Lost Son* contained the poems "Child on Top of a Greenhouse," "Orchids," and "A Field of Light." Roethke called the greenhouses "a universe, several

The Saginaw house in which poet Theodore Roethke spent his childhood is now in the care of a nonprofit society dedicated to his memory and works. A state historical marker designates the site. Photo by David Riddick.

worlds, which, even as a child, one worried about, and struggled to keep alive."

"In these green images, Roethke reached the center of his memory and found his wholly individual idiom," wrote Louis Martz in "A Greenhouse Eden."[1] "On a mission of self-discovery, Roethke regresses into his own past to rediscover his beginnings—a sort of going back in order to go forward." John Boyd said readers often found most representative of his work the greenhouse poems and others "about orchids and geraniums, about bats, night crows, field mice and summer storms."[2] As Roethke told the *Saginaw News* in 1949, "Any serious writer uses the imagery he saw and heard and felt about him as a youth. This is the imagery most vivid to him. It becomes symbolic."

Roethke began his writing career before family disaster struck. At thirteen, his speech about the Junior Red Cross received favorable attention. A hungry reader, he wrote for the student newspaper at Saginaw Arthur

Hill High School. His appetite extended to whiskey. He joined an illegal fraternity and consumed bootleg products, in part to win social acceptance. He also became an enthusiastic and competitive tennis player. He is said to have limped onto the court, feigning an injury, to lure his opponent into complacency.

A row between his father Otto and uncle Charles led to the sale of the greenhouses. Shortly afterward, Otto was diagnosed with cancer and Charles took his own life. When Otto passed away, Theodore became at age fifteen the nominal head of the household. But he would write of his yearning for his father in some of his most memorable poetry.

The yearning wasn't a simple paean to a benign parent. Otto was fierce, short-tempered, and sometimes intolerant of his son's occasional clumsiness. Theodore wrote of not being able to live up to his father's desire to make him "a wise fisherman and a self-sufficient woodsman." He remembered a trip to Houghton Lake to fish pike and bass. He woke up late, forgot some of his tackle, rowed poorly, and knocked his father's hat off. "The next day I wasn't asked to go along. It was a hard blow."

Otto's death at age fifty-two deprived the two of the chance to reconcile fully, and for the son to win his father's approval as a nationally known poet. But the memory of the father appears in Theodore's poetry, a bittersweet blend of love and sometimes painful candor and longing. In Roethke's *My Papa's Waltz*, published in 1942, are two revealing stanzas:

The whiskey on your breath
Could make a small boy dizzy
But I hung on like death:
Such waltzing was not easy

You beat time on my head
With a palm caked hard by dirt,
Then waltzed me off to bed
Still clinging to your shirt.

Roethke and his mother Helen had an uneasy relationship after Otto's death. At her insistence, he attended the University of Michigan, preparing for a legal career. He graduated magna cum laude in 1929, but quit law school after a semester. He spent two years taking graduate classes at the university and later at Harvard. In 1931, economic pressures forced him to discontinue his graduate studies and begin teaching English and coaching tennis at Pennsylvania's Lafayette College, where he remained until 1935.

That autumn, he began teaching at what was then Michigan State College in East Lansing. But in mid-November, he suffered a nervous breakdown that resulted in a two-month stay at a sanitarium. The college released him from his teaching position.

Saginaw was a refuge for Roethke in his adulthood, just as it had been a refuge for wildlife on the family's preserve. Through his thirties, he frequently returned to his hometown to renew himself and refine his poetry.

Recovery from his 1935 breakdown was robust enough to enable Roethke to obtain a master's degree in fine arts from the University of Michigan and begin teaching English composition and poetry at Penn State University. He also coached the school's tennis team for five years. Thirty-three years old in 1941, he published his first book of poetry, *Open House*, the culmination of ten years of work. Robert Frost was one of the many who acclaimed Roethke as an original and powerful American voice.

Recognition and honors proliferated. Roethke became the youngest poet to read at Harvard's annual Morris Gray Series in 1942. He also became one of three judges for the American College Quill Club's National Poetry Contest.

In 1943, Roethke began teaching at Bennington College while working on his next volume of poetry. He suffered a second breakdown, for which he received electroshock therapy that terrified him.

The University of Michigan Press in 1946 published ten Roethke poems in *New Michigan Verse*. Long eager to join the university's faculty, Roethke applied for a teaching job that year. But the English department chair, aware of Roethke's second breakdown in 1945, thought him too "unstable" to hire. The university recognized its mistake when, in 1962, it awarded Roethke an honorary doctorate at the same time it awarded one to Robert Frost.

A growing critical reputation and strong recommendations from colleagues at Bennington resulted in a lasting faculty appointment as an associate professor of English at the University of Washington in 1947. In his recommendation letter to the University of Washington, the former president of Bennington College, Lewis Jones, wrote, "He is an extremely complex, temperamental and somewhat eccentric person . . . If the University of Washington can take his eccentric personality, it will acquire one of the best teachers I have ever seen."

The lushness of the Pacific Northwest brought out the poet's reverence for nature. "He absorbed an awful lot from the wildness around Seattle simply by sitting in it, or walking a short way in it, and becoming a part of it," writer David Wagoner said in a 2005 documentary, *I Remember Thedore Roethke*, produced by Seattle filmmaker Jean Walkinshaw.

Roethke published a second collection of poetry, *The Lost Son and Other Poems*, in 1948, and a third, *Praise to the End*, in 1951. The early 1950s brought Roethke a Guggenheim Fellowship award and *Poetry Magazine*'s Levinson Prize, as well as grants from the Ford Foundation and the National Institute of Arts and Letters. His fourth volume, *The Waking: Poems, 1933–1953*, won a Pulitzer Prize in poetry in 1954.

Well-known as a dallier with his female students as well as an alcoholic and epicure, the poet married Beatrice O'Connell, whom he had taught at Bennington, in January 1953. She was devoted to him, but life with a man characterized today as bipolar could not have been easy. In the 2005 documentary, Beatrice remembered: "His depression didn't bother me. In fact one day he said, 'You'll be happy to hear I was mildly depressed today.' But his manic phases were very upsetting."

The poem "In a Dark Time" refers to his exquisite torment:

What's madness but nobility of soul
At odds with circumstance. The day's on fire!
I know the purity of pure despair.

Words for the Wind, published in 1957, won the Bollingen Prize, the National Book Award, the Longview Foundation Award, the Edna St. Vincent Millay Prize, and the Pacific Northwest Writer's Award. Reputedly notified of his Bollingen award while teaching a class, Roethke is said to have exclaimed, "To the Moon!" The Blue Moon Tavern was one of Roethke's favorites nearby. A painting of the poet still hangs there.

A biographer described another classroom scene from Roethke's time at what was then known as Michigan State College. The poet told his class,

"Now you watch what I do for the next five minutes and describe it." The teacher then climbed out on a narrow ledge that girdled the building about ten feet off the ground. He crept around the building, making faces at each window before climbing back in.[3]

Roethke balanced his teaching and writing careers with reading tours in Europe and New York. In 1955 and 1956, the Roethkes traveled in Italy, Europe, and England on his Fulbright grant. He later did reading tours in New York and Europe.

On August 1, 1963, during a visit to the estate of friends Prentice and Virginia Bloedel on Washington's Bainbridge Island, he suffered a fatal heart attack and died in a swimming pool. One story in island lore holds that Roethke sat by the pool that summer afternoon, fixing mint juleps. Another holds that he rewarded himself with a drink each time he completed a lap. When Virginia Bloedel returned from to the main house after an errand, Roethke was floating face down in the water. Three perfect mint juleps, it is said, sat on a table by the edge of the pool.

The Bloedels filled the pool with soil and created a Zen rock garden as a memorial to Roethke. Another memorial came in the form of sixty-one new poems found and published posthumously in 1964's *The Far Field*, and in *The Collected Poems*, published in 1966.

According to renowned poet and author Rosemary Sullivan, Roethke's poetry conveys "his sensitivity to the subliminal, irrational world of nature; his relationship to his dead father, who occupies the center of his work . . . his attempts to explore other modes of consciousness which carried him to the edge of psychic disaster . . . his interest in mysticism . . . his debts, so well repaid, to the poetic ancestors from whom he learned his craft; and the calm joyousness which rests at the core of his work."

In the November 1968 *Atlantic*, James Dickey stated: "There is no poetry anywhere that is so valuably conscious of the human body as Roethke's; no poetry that can place the body in an environment." Roethke is considered to be an influence on poets James Dickey, Robert Bly, Sylvia Plath, and Anne Sexton.

Roethke came home one last time. He is buried in Oakwood Cemetery in Saginaw Township. His namesake foundation awards the Theodore M. Roethke Poetry Prize every three years, accompanied by a $3,000 check.

At a 2008 Saginaw observance of Roethke's centenary, his widow, now living in England, provided greetings in a letter: "[Ted] would have been amused, astonished and deeply touched that people in Saginaw are celebrating his birthday."

Works (of Poetry)

Open House (New York: A.A. Knopf, 1941).
The Lost Son and Other Poems (Garden City, NY: Doubleday, 1948).
Words for the Wind (London: Secker & Warburg, 1947).
Praise to the End!, 1st ed. (Garden City, NY: Doubleday, 1951).
The Waking: Poems, 1933–1955 (Garden City, NY: Doubleday, 1953).
I Am! Says the Lamb (Garden City, NY: Doubleday, 1961).
Party at the Zoo (New York: Crowell-Collier Press, 1963).
The Far Field (London: Faber & Faber, 1964).
The Collected Poems of Theodore Roethke (Seattle: University of Washington Press, 1966).

Sites

Theodore Roethke Boyhood Home, 1805 Gratiot, Saginaw, Michigan
Theodore Roethke Grave, 6100 Gratiot, Saginaw, Michigan

Maritta Wolff

Sudden Fame

December 25, 1918–July 1, 2002
Born near Grass Lake; wrote three best-selling novels with Michigan backdrops

- -

A writer's first and last volumes are literally bookends. In the case of Michigan's Maritta Wolff, those works are also the towers of a career bridge spanning seventy-four years. Coming out of nowhere to author one of the most talked-about American bestsellers of 1941, *Whistle Stop*, she also received favorable national critical attention for her posthumous *Sudden Rain* in 2005.

What nurtured an artistic sensibility able to capture what critics of the time called the "sordid" and "vulgar" in human nature? The wellspring of Maritta Wolff's art was a childhood near Grass Lake. Today, in part a bedroom town for commuters to Jackson and Ann Arbor, Grass Lake was in the 1920s and 1930s a self-contained—and in Wolff's keen gaze, isolated—small community on the Detroit-Chicago rail line.

Born out of wedlock on Christmas Day, 1918, Wolff was the daughter of a young local woman and a newspaper/novelist father. Growing up on her grandparents' farm near Grass Lake, she applied discerning scrutiny to

Disappointed by her agent's handling of what turned out to be her final manuscript, Maritta Wolff put it in her refrigerator. It stayed there until after her death more than thirty years later, when it was published as *Sudden Rain* and attracted a favorable review from the *New York Times.* Courtesy of Hugh Stegman.

family and small-town life, perhaps in part because of town gossip about her unmarried parents. During those years she also formed a strong, lifelong attachment to her mother, to whom she was devoted.

Grass Lake had a vital connection to the larger world: the Michigan Central railroad. In one of Wolff's novels, a character finds a chance for a second life after being hauled aboard a passing freight train. Other characters dreamt of such an escape. Significantly, one of the most memorable events in the history of Grass Lake was the 1902 crash of two trains in a Thanksgiving snowstorm.

Her childhood was lonely, Wolff later recalled. She said she "seldom played with other children" and attended a one-room rural school. "It would be nice if I could say I walked two miles to school every day, but if I remember correctly it was only half a mile that I walked."

Wolff enrolled at the University of Michigan after graduation from the Grass Lake high school. Intending to study journalism but ending up an English major, she ultimately received a degree in composition and a Phi Beta Kappa key. She won two small Hopwood prizes for short stories, which paid some of her college expenses. She then produced an 830-page manuscript for a composition class. It captured the university's 1940 Avery Hopwood Prize for writing. It also caught a publisher's eye, and in a 450-page redraft, became a 1941 blockbuster.

Whistle Stop is a story of the struggling, squabbling Veech family in a small town not unlike Grass Lake. Its most memorable characters are the charming, shambling party boy Freddy; his beautiful, superficially aloof sister Mary; and the clan's matriarch, Molly. Mother and grandmother to a complex family, the rotund Molly fights to hold the family together in the midst of calamities she seems not to fathom—alcoholism, infidelity, incest, dementia, and sociopathy.

The book shocked critics and readers because of both its subject matter and the age of its author. How, they asked, could a twenty-three-year-old have acquired such penetrating insight into human complexity, and how could she render dialogue so realistically and faithfully that one reviewer called it "scientifically exact"?

Wolff provided one explanation early in her career. "My one hobby was developing, as far back as I can remember, even under the handicap of my somewhat isolated life in the country, an inordinate interest in people and everything happening to them."

The result was good enough to win praise from Nobel Prize–winning author Sinclair Lewis, also a chronicler of the depths beneath the surface of small-town Midwestern life. Commenting on *Whistle Stop*, he tagged Wolff as a writer to watch, saying she "writes the seamy side of life with glittering skill and a brutal, brawling, turbulent sense of character and human drama." He called the book the most important novel of the year. And in a letter to Wolff about *Night Shift*, her second novel, he advised her to ignore critics' comments: "This is all God damned idiocy . . . You're a grand novelist!"

Grass Lake presumably provides the backdrop for the fictional small town of *Whistle Stop*. To find refuge, the Veeches' youngest son, Fred, takes an evening summer stroll:

> Out on the street the fresh air drove the sickness and dizziness out of him. He walked away from the blatant band music and the lights and the high wooden bandstand set up in the middle of the street, amid the clutter of automobiles and people. He walked along the dark quiet streets with his face lifted to the trees and to the clean sky overhead where the first pale stars shone. Beyond the railroad tracks the lake water shone a little among the weeds and the trees and bushes, and the frogs and the crickets and all of the other voices of the night sang louder here. In spite of himself, Carl's nerves relaxed.

The Grass Lake train station is the symbol of escape from a small town's limits for one of the chief characters in Maritta Wolff's debut novel, *Whistle Stop*. Considered "vulgar" by some critics, the frank novel sold briskly, exposing human nature in a small town not unlike Grass Lake. Photo by Jack Dempsey.

In *Whistle Stop*, Wolff renders American speech in the tradition of Twain. One monologue also seems to prefigure the famous Brando speech from *On the Waterfront*:

> I get so sick of this, I just can't stand it. I wasn't never cut out for railroading. I got brains. I could get some place if I got outa this town. The thing is, I never had a chance. I never even got a chance to go to high school. Soon as I got big enough I had to quit school and start working.

New Yorker critic Clifton Fadiman contrasted Wolff's background with her ruthlessly realistic fiction. "If her English composition entitled *Whistle Stop* counts as evidence, she did not learn her trade in the college classroom. Miss Wolff knows too many things not discoverable around any college campus." It was remarkable that "a Michigan farm girl" could write about sex, crime, and violence, he said.

Not surprisingly, the Grass Lake community didn't know what to do with its young celebrity. Some were pleased with being known as the home of a talented new literary sensation. Others in Grass Lake kept her at arm's length, suspicious that Wolff was mocking its people and way of life. There was no doubt, however, that she was describing their town—its two church spires, the water tower, the old road bed over which the interurban passed on its way through the village on its way between Jackson and Detroit, its weedy lake at the outskirts, and Wednesday night band concerts on the main street.

The *Grass Lake News* noted the unease but came down on the side of the author. While noting that some local residents "have been slow to place their stamp of approval" on *Whistle Stop*, the newspaper was pleased that the small town was getting national advertising. "Whether we place our approval on the book or not, the fact remains that Miss Wolff has written a story—a modern story in the accepted modern style—which is the sensation of the nation."

Outside the little community, readers responded to ads for the $2.50 hardcover. "Discovered" was the banner on one advertisement. The discoverers of "The New Avery Hopwood Prize Novel," besides Lewis, included a "famed book assayer" from the *American News*, Donald Gordon, who called it "a stopper . . . A genuine talent has come over the whole."

The encore novel, *Night Shift*, followed in 1942. A *New York Times* review praised the book's description and dialogue of automobile-bumper plant workers, taxi drivers, greasy-spoon waitresses, and "beautiful dumb women and beautiful smart ones who haunt small-time night clubs." The setting of *Night Shift* is a mid-sized industrial town like the Jackson, Michigan, of the early 1940s. The grinding, grumbling sounds of auto plants and supplier factories are almost always audible in the background. In the foreground are worker injuries and a death in one of those factories, a mental hospital where a man languishes in borderline insanity, and the tiny boarding house on Horton Street in which Sally, one of the main characters—like Molly in *Whistle Stop*—somehow provides a functioning habitat for her siblings and children. At the same time, a sad elderly widow upstairs evokes the unhappiness of life gone awry. Another central character, Sally's sister—a "working girl" who sings in a local nightclub—unexpectedly falls for an inscrutable, seemingly sociopathic lover.

These two early novels became films, after adulteration. *Whistle Stop* starred George Raft and the young Ava Gardner; the other, entitled *The Man I Love*, based on *Night Shift*, featured Ida Lupino. Reviewers were cynical. One called *The Man I Love* "silly and depressing, not to mention downright dull." The Hollywood sausage-making machine lost its appeal for author Wolff.

Those who thought, based on her early works, that Wolff must be brassy and tough-talking were surprised. After Wolff's third book, *About Lyddy Thomas*, in 1948, a Pennsylvania writer who met her said, "She is very light, and very thin, with long reddish-blonde hair. And she is either shy, or reserved to the point, practically, of being all-reserved. The last thing you would expect of her is the achievement of two best-sellers."[1]

The author described her writing routine: sleep in the daytime and work at night free from distractions, family time on weekends, and back to the typewriter after Monday dinner. The characters, she said, had their own will and led her in directions she never anticipated.

While a student at the University of Michigan, Wolff met and married another novelist, Hubert Skidmore. Their marriage was stormy. An alcoholic, Skidmore returned from World War II service with what is now called post-traumatic stress disorder. He died in a house fire after falling asleep smoking one night in February 1946.

In the 1950s, Wolff moved to the Los Angeles area. She published three novels after *About Lyddy Thomas*, working through 1962, then apparently fell silent the rest of her life before passing away in 2002. But typically for Wolff, the story was not so simple.

Tucked away in her Los Angeles kitchen refrigerator was a manuscript she had completed in the early 1970s, but never published. Although her obituaries said she had shelved it because her publisher had demanded promotional appearances the shy Wolff had not wanted to make, family members said her ire resulted from the first manuscript rejection of her career. Outraged, she decided not to market it to another publisher and gave up the writing of novels—but preserved the last, thinking a fire would not destroy the contents of her refrigerator.

The author's voice was irrepressible even after death, however. Her family took the manuscript to Scribner, which published it in 2005 as *Sudden Rain*. Set in the early 1970s, *Sudden Rain* depicts the flailing of two generations trying to come to terms with runaway cultural change, against the backdrop of the Pacific Palisades of Southern California. Troubled modern marriages are a central feature of the novel. Her own second marriage, to Leonard Stegman, was not a success; the two spent their final decades separated, although still amicable.

Critics took notice of *Sudden Rain*. Janet Maslin of the *New York Times* said the novel preserved a cultural Pompeii of American life "flawlessly in literary lava." *Publishers Weekly* described it as "a brilliant, noirish cultural commentary."

The novel is especially sympathetic to women slipping out of the strait-jacket of conventional roles. Wolff carries forward into her final published novel the view of culturally destroyed female potential that first starred in *Whistle Stop*. Her view of men is similarly critical. One female character observes of her son-in-law: "Not that she had anything against Jack personally: Actually she adored him, she always thought he was an absolute doll. It was just that he was a man, and like the best of them, he had the curious potential to turn into the most complete bastard given half a chance."

Again, the writer's style and choice of subject matter did not represent her character as others knew her. Her family and friends found her warm, thoughtful, and funny, and scores of correspondents, including many fans, received detailed and grateful notes in return. Christmas was her favorite holiday because she enjoyed shopping for, and giving, gifts chosen with just the right touch for their recipients. When it came to the troubled side of life and human nature, "her novels were her voice" and all she had to say, according to her daughter-in-law Laura Stegman.

In her eighth decade, Maritta Wolff made one of her few pilgrimages to the town of her youth. The occasion was the 1992 dedication of the restored railroad depot that had helped make Grass Lake "a whistle stop." By that time, with her initial novel out of print and difficult to find, the city's leaders may have been unaware that the book illuminated what Sinclair Lewis had called "the seamy side" of its people and ways. Wolff rode among locals on an Amtrak train from Ann Arbor that made a special stop in Grass Lake to commemorate the depot's rededication. As downtown boosters reported, "The title of Maritta's novel was the inspiration for naming the organization that owns the depot and [an adjacent] park." The depot is still one of the attractions promoted by the town.

Readers who rededicate themselves to the works of Wolff will find a supreme storytelling talent worth far more attention than she receives today—and a look at the grit of small town and industrial life in Michigan during the first half of the twentieth century, as well as the upheavals of American society during its second half, in a metropolis two thousand miles west.

Works

Whistle Stop (New York: Random House, 1941).
Night Shift (New York: Random House, 1942).
About Lyddy Thomas (New York: Random House, 1943).
Back of Town (New York: Random House, 1952).
The Big Nickelodeon (New York: Random House, 1956).
Buttonwood (New York: Random House, 1962).
Sudden Rain (New York: Scribner, 2005).

Sites

Grass Lake Depot and Whistle Stop Park, 210 East Michigan Avenue, Grass Lake, Michigan

Southwest Michigan

Liberty Hyde Bailey

A Bountiful Life

March 15, 1858–December 25, 1954

Born in South Haven; graduate of Michigan Agricultural College and chairman of its Horticulture Department

Descended from a Revolutionary War veteran, Liberty Hyde Bailey was given his father's name as a political statement on the eve of the American Civil War. Rooted in the freedom-loving soil of West Michigan, that name could not have been more apt as testimony against the evil of involuntary servitude. His long lifetime would be devoted to fashioning a more bounteous world for urban and rural dwellers, men and women, adults and children. Among his many accomplishments was helping establish the academic discipline of landscape architecture. He coined the botanical terms "cultivar," "cultigen," and "indigen." The Michigan-originated "Red Haven peach," a modern pinnacle of the fruit, owes its existence to his South Haven origins. He was, in sum, a creative genius born from the fertile loam of the Great Lakes State.

And he wrote. Over eight decades, Bailey authored or edited more than two hundred books and seven hundred papers, including a 1,000-page monograph (*Rubus in North America*) that he published in 1945 and, learning of necessary additions, supplemented in 1947 and 1949. Of the books, six dealt with philosophy and one with poetry; the remainder were studies in horticulture-related subjects. Many are still in print, and his favorite, *The Holy Earth*, a fifteen-volume work on the philosophy of rural life, was reprinted in 1980 for the third time. He edited several multivolume publications, such as *The Cyclopedia of American Agriculture* (1907–1909) and the *Cyclopedia of American Horticulture* (1900–1902), as well as the *Rural Science, Rural Textbook, Gardencraft*, and *Young Folks Library* series of manuals.

L. H. Bailey was an antebellum baby, born on March 15, 1858, in the port hamlet of South Haven, the third child of pioneers who cleared a patch of land out of unbroken forest not far from the big lake in order to farm for their subsistence. The decision to homestead there was propitious: southwest Michigan is one of the world's lushest habitats. Adjacent to the Lake Michigan shore, the land is blessed by moderate temperatures and abundant moisture. South Haven was formed at the mouth of the Black River, a natural site for shipping lumber, a safe place to put in during lake storms, and beginning in the late 1800s, an easy destination for Chicago excursionists seeking to escape summer heat. Picture-postcard sunsets have drawn tourists and beach-goers ever since.

Life for L.H. was no Garden of Eden, though. His mother died when he was four, leaving him to the care of his father, older brother, and, eventually, stepmother. Still, his mother's influence surpassed their brief time together, for she introduced her son to the love of growing things by involving him in her garden planting. South Haven being just a village, Bailey attended a one-room country school, where he benefited from another key female influence. His teacher introduced him to the classics of literature and Darwin's *The Origin of Species*. These books led him to begin studying plant life and the birds, insects, and rodents so prevalent in the country around his farm home and school.

As he grew beyond adolescence, Bailey began to make his mark on the community. He invented a classification system to organize studies of nature. He learned how to graft quality stock in the fruit orchards that blossomed on the surrounding hills and lowlands, a skill that made him indispensable to neighbors. When he was only fifteen, Bailey wrote and presented a paper

L. H. Bailey emerged from boyhood amid the farms and orchards of southwest Michigan to write and teach a new comprehension of the natural world. His long career began at the agricultural college in East Lansing. Courtesy of Michigan State University Archives and Historical Collections (People, Bailey, Liberty Hyde, no. 133).

entitled "Bird" at the South Haven Pomological Society meeting.[1] The work was so enthusiastically received that he was invited to present it to the state Pomological Society meeting in September 1873. Its publication in the society's annual report also earned him election as the South Haven branch's first ornithologist.

During these early years while out in the field, Bailey met a botanist from New York, Lucy Millington, who was touring the area. She took him along on collecting trips and presented him at visit's end with her plant-collecting case, a memento of their explorations together. Yet another female mentor had found something important to nurture in the young man. Millington's influence led Liberty to think of horizons beyond the west Michigan shore.

In 1877, at the age of nineteen, he borrowed $10 from the South Haven Bank, wrapped his clothes in a carpet remnant, and took the train to East Lansing to enroll at Michigan Agricultural College. All good Michigan farm boys yearned to attend the school to advance in their trade. His foremost mentor was Professor William J. Beal, a former student of leading American

The South Haven house and park-like grounds of Liberty Hyde Bailey's youth now comprise a museum in the care of a local nonprofit society. A state historical marker also designates the site. Photo by Jack Dempsey.

botanist Asa Gray. The latter's *Field, Forest, and Garden Botany* had been one of Bailey's favorite books in his one-room school days at South Haven. Professor Beal was a pioneer in the laboratory method of teaching botany: he did not rely merely on book learning, but immersed his students in "hands-on" experiences, a learning technique that inspired Bailey as an instructor. He soon embarked on that career. While yet an MAC student, Bailey took his first teaching position at the Carl School, a one-room schoolhouse at the corner of Saginaw and Pine Lake (now Lake Lansing) Roads in East Lansing, both to earn money and because he enjoyed educating others.

Bailey also began to write deliberately. He became editor of *The College Speculum*, MAC's first student newspaper. The periodical published his opinion pieces focused on the need for a practical agricultural education similar to what he had experienced in Beal's botany classes. In 1880 the *Botanical Gazette* published his article "Michigan Lake Shore Plants." Student, teacher, editor, writer: Bailey was beginning a career in words.

Attending MAC had other benefits, for here he met and married Annette Smith, daughter of a Michigan farmer. Graduating in 1882, he briefly served as a newspaper reporter at the *Springfield (Illinois) Morning Monitor.* It appeared as if journalism would be his bent. Beal would not leave him there. With his mentor's encouragement, Bailey entered Harvard and, in late 1882, made his way into Asa Gray's employment as an assistant in charge of nomenclature for gardens, greenhouses, and herbaria. And Beal would not leave him there, either.

In 1885, Beal managed an invitation from MAC for Bailey to return as chairman of the Horticulture Department. The school was launching a newly organized discipline that included landscape gardening, the first program of its kind in the country. Bailey accepted; a year later, while serving in its administration, he also received an MS degree from the college. In 1888 he led design and construction of the nation's first horticulture laboratory. Eustace Hall was specifically constructed for Bailey and his department. He used it as a base from which to travel widely through the state, teaching, lecturing, and studying. His reputation was spreading beyond Michigan.

In 1888 he left MAC for a position at Cornell University as professor and chairman of practical and experimental horticulture. The title was the first at an American university, and it led to the position of dean of the College of Agriculture. In 1894, his renown gained him a singular honor: he was asked to revise the classic volume he had loved so much as a boy—Gray's *Field, Forest, and Garden Botany*—stamping his own mark on the work by more than doubling the plants detailed.

During his early tenure at Cornell, the economic dislocation of the 1890s caused many Americans to leave family farms for what they saw as a more stable life in the city. Bailey fought the tide. He began publishing the "Home Nature Study Course" and authored his first leaflet, *How a Squash Plant Gets Out of the Seed,* trying to encourage perseverance in U.S. agricultural pursuits. Cornell offered a Nature Study School in the summer of 1897. Bailey, with others, organized Junior Naturalist Clubs and began publishing the *Junior Naturalist Monthly* in 1899. He wrote a series of books for all ages on plants and nature, *Lessons with Plants* (1898), an elementary school textbook (1900), a beginner's book (1908), and a secondary text (1913), all to educate and inspire its readers about the virtues of rural life. His "Rural School

Leaflets" resulted in the formation of farm-based Boys and Girls Clubs, the forerunner of 4-H clubs. In 1901 he became editor of *Country Life in America*, published by Doubleday, the purpose of which was to acknowledge that

> we may in a measure gravitate to the cities, but our country dwellers are not to be forgotten, . . . [with a goal to have each edition] reflect the particular season of the year in relation to a section of country. Naturally the garden and its cultivation will form topics of the greatest interest. But the decorative portion of life in the country will not alone be shown, for there are the practical ends of a country's existence.[2]

In 1907, Bailey was a featured invitee to the 50th anniversary celebration at MAC, and once more he returned to the East Lansing campus that had been his second home. His address was on "The State and the Farmer." A co-speaker, Teddy Roosevelt, was so impressed by the talk that the 26th president of the United States invited the scholar out to dinner afterward. As the conversation unfolded, the president enlisted Bailey in a new effort to save an old way of life. Roosevelt was equally concerned about the state of rural America, and he was creating a Commission on Country Life to investigate why increasing numbers of people were leaving the farm, and what to do about it. Bailey chaired the commission, which included other luminaries such as Gifford Pinchot, conservationist and first director of the U.S. Forest Service. He earnestly dove into the work, guiding the commission to seek the widest advice, proof of which can be found in a letter received from W.E.B. Du Bois urging the commission not to ignore the plight of rural Southern blacks. The ensuing report was a landmark, finding that rural communities suffered from underinvestment, inadequate schools, poor roads, and lagging communication networks. Because rural Americans felt isolated and unappreciated, they needed attention—all of them.

It was, after all, the age of Progressivism. Roosevelt's formation of the commission and the choice of Bailey to head it were in keeping with the era, but out of this came a movement of its own. Bailey authored the book that reflected its reform agenda, entitled *The Country Life Movement in the U.S.* The goal, as Bailey framed it, was as enormous as "the working out of the desire to make rural civilization as effective and satisfying as other civilization." It was essential to achieve this end for all rural people, not just a portion of the population. Bailey called for educational opportunity on behalf of all who sought to better themselves:

> I would not limit the entrance of women into any courses of the College of Agriculture; on the contrary, I want all courses open to them freely and on equal terms with men . . . Furthermore I do not conceive it to be essential that all teachers in home economics subjects be women; nor, on the other hand, do I think it is essential that all teachers in the other series of departments shall be men. The person who is best qualified to teach the subjects should be the one who teaches it . . . I hope for the time when there will be as many women in the College of Agriculture as there are men.

Perhaps the memory of three women who were vital to his intellectual advancement as a young boy had inspired these words.

Perhaps, too, his service on the commission led him to a new line of inquiry. Bailey left academia, and his writing became more philosophical. Aboard a ship to New Zealand in 1914, he wrote *The Holy Earth* on scraps of paper, envelopes, and backs of letters. "The book is not a nature-study manual nor a 'rhapsody on the beauties of nature, but a questioning of man's basic relation to the earth and to his fellow man.' It summed up Bailey's philosophy—that a righteous use of the vast resources of the earth must be founded on religious and ethical values."[3] One passage expressed a deeply spiritual side of someone often regarded as a purely scientific writer:

> If the earth is holy, then the things that grow out of the earth are also holy. They do not belong to man to do with them as he will. Dominion does not carry personal ownership. There are many generations of folk yet to come after us, who will have equal right with us to the products of the globe. It would seem that a divine obligation rests on every soul. Are we to make righteous use of the vast accumulation of knowledge of the planet? If so, we must have a new formulation. The partition of the earth among the millions who live on it is necessarily a question of morals; and a society that is founded on an unmoral partition and use cannot itself be righteous and whole.

Another carried the ecological thought to an elevated plane:

> It is good to live. We talk of death and of lifelessness, but we know only of life. Even our prophecies of death are prophecies of more life. We know no better world: whatever else there may be is of things hoped for, not of things seen.

The Holy Earth was followed by a collection of poems entitled *Wind and Weather* (in 1916), then a series of general topic volumes under the titles *Universal Service* and *What Is Democracy?* (both in 1918), *The Apple Tree* (1922), *The Seven Stars* (1923), *The Harvest of the Year* (1927), and *The Garden Lover* (1928). These so-called "background books" advanced the tradition of Thoreau and Burroughs, yet had their own style because of Bailey's scientific background. His writing skill so impressed George P. Brett, president of Macmillan and Co., that he committed the company to publishing whatever Bailey would write. In total, almost one million copies of Bailey's works were sold.

This latest phase was not an accident. As a teenager, L. H. Bailey laid out a plan for his life. He would spend a quarter century learning horticulture and the natural world, the next twenty-five years in earning his livelihood, and the final twenty-five using his abilities as he saw fit. And he carried out that plan. The final phase lasted longer than projected:

> Lively and strong-minded, Dr. Bailey thought nothing at 91 of making a trip to the West Indies to search for palms. He did that in April, 1949. A huge birthday party planned for him by Cornell University—he was dean emeritus of its College of Agriculture—had to be postponed because he was wandering through the jungles.[4]

That long life finally came to an end in his ninety-sixth year—though true to form, even the date, Christmas Day, carried meaning, as had so much of his preceding 35,000 days. The *New York Times* obituary declared him an "internationally renowned botanist, horticulturist and agricultural educator" and recounted:

> Until the end, he frequently was showered with honors. He believed one should accept conditions as they were, not let money be the primary motivation, but keep as a chief aim the artistic expression of life.

Bailey was buried in Lakeview Cemetery in Ithaca, the New York college town he had helped put on the map.

Artistic expression found itself in his teaching, his writing, and also his photography, an activity enjoyed until death. He left behind an international reputation as one of the five founding members of the Botanical Society of London, a member of the American Philosophical Society, and the recipient of not only the Veitch gold and silver medals from the Royal Horticultural Society in London, but also a diploma of honor from the Royal Botanical Gardens in Denmark. In the United States, he received an honorary LLD from the University of Wisconsin and an honorary LittD from the University of Vermont. Bailey bridged science and philosophy, seeking to link humanity to nature, to connect all persons to their natural environment:

> Men can be classified by the profession or field of activity whereby they achieved their greatness; not so with Liberty Hyde Bailey, for his greatness is due to his manifold contributions produced almost concurrently in many fields. To some persons, his renown is as a botanist, explorer, and horticulturist; to others as an educator, administrator and rural sociologist; to a third group as an editor, lecturer, and writer; while still a fourth group knows him best as a poet, philosopher, and counselor. He was all these things, and moreover, he was a man of forceful character, personality and energy.[5]

Today, his childhood home is a museum located at, appropriately, 903 Bailey Avenue in South Haven. The circa 1856 house, oldest residential structure in town, is a quaint two-story white clapboard frame structure with a pillared porch, generous gables, hidden features, and well-manicured grounds on what is left of the original 80-acre Bailey fruit farm. The smokehouse and carriage barn still stand. Back in the day, some two thousand fruit trees covered half of the farm, and the remainder produced grain, vegetable, sorghum, and livestock products. Thrice it was recognized as the best commercial Michigan apple orchard in the 1870s. The state historical marker in front says: "Here in wilderness surroundings he learned of wild animals and plants and attended the local village school." A local marker describes him as "South Haven's most distinguished son."

His alma mater did not forget him either. The site of his horticulture laboratory on the East Lansing campus is the first building at MSU listed on the

National Register of Historic Places. Eustace Hall, red brick and clapboard sided and the third-oldest building on campus, serves as headquarters for the Honors College—given Bailey's academic record, an appropriate home. MSU further honored his memory by creating the Bailey Scholars program for agriculture and natural-science scholars.

His literary standing does not rank as high:

> Taken as a whole, Liberty Hyde Bailey's works can be considered a buried treasure whose rediscovery is long overdue. Liberty Bailey believed ardently in a democracy that rested upon the self-confidence, public spirit, and civic skills of ordinary people and in a government that worked in partnership with the people to produce things of public value. Bailey continued Abraham Lincoln's vision of a "new birth of freedom," founded in popular self-governance. This again is the task of our age.[6]

The scientific community, though, has always treasured him. When the American Society for Horticultural Science initiated a worldwide Hall of Fame in 1990, they inducted only two individuals in the first class: Gregor Mendel, the Austrian who invented plant hybridization, and Bailey. Notably, his stature derived in large part from his writing: "As author, editor, teacher, and frequent public speaker, Bailey helped create the science of horticulture."[7]

Less appreciated for his writing, he is little known today beyond academic circles. The fruit orchards blanketing the Southwest Michigan hills all the way to the vineyards on the Old Mission Peninsula might be described as Bailey Country. Lake-moderated breezes nurture trees and shrubs bursting with produce. And if production itself were not enough, the landscape all up and down the West Michigan shore surely would delight Bailey today, with field upon sun-embraced field reaching as far as the eye can see.

Bailey's ego never outgrew the humble setting of his childhood:

> I do not yet know why plants come out of the land or float in streams, or creep on rocks or roll from the sea. I am entranced by the mystery of them, and absorbed by their variety and kinds. Everywhere they are visible yet everywhere occult.

He never lost his fascination with the natural world—discovering new plants, or determining how to keep farmers more in tune with the land they should love. Bailey had no such lack, having grown up in the embrace of the family farm. This experience deeply influenced him throughout his long life, for he would vouch that his writings "all came out of South Haven. My roots are here and my experiences here must enter into my consciousness. All life comes out of childhood." Growing from the fertile West Michigan soil, the life it yielded would enrich many a printed page.

Works[8]

Field Notes on Apple Culture (New York: Orange Judd Co., 1886).

The Garden Fence (Boston: Wright & Potter Co., 1886).

Talks A-Field: About Plants and the Science of Plants (New York: Rural Publishing Co., 1887).

Horticulturist's Rule-Book: A Compendium of Useful Information for Fruit-Growers, Truck-Gardeners, Florists, and Others (New York: Rural Publishing Co., 1890).

Annals of Horticulture in North America for the Year 1889: A Witness of Passing Events and a Record of Progress (New York: Rural Publishing Co., 1890).

The Nursery-Book: A Complete Guide to the Multiplication and Pollination of Plants (New York: Rural Publishing Co., 1891).

Annals of Horticulture in North America for the Year 1890 (New York: Rural Publishing Co., 1891).

Cross-Breeding and Hybridizing (New York: Rural Publishing Co., 1892).

American Grape Training; An Account of the Leading Forms Now in Use of Training American Grapes (New York: Rural Publishing Co., 1893).

Annals of Horticulture in North America for the Year 1892 (New York: Rural Publishing, 1893).

Annals of Horticulture in North America for the Year 1893 (New York: Orange Judd Co., 1894).

Plant-Breeding: Being Six Lectures upon the Amelioration of Domestic Plants (New York and London: Macmillan, 1895).

The Survival of the Unlike: A Collection of Evolution Essays Suggested by the Study of Domestic Plants (New York: Macmillan, 1896).

The Forcing Book: A Manual of the Cultivation of Vegetables in Glass Houses (New York: Macmillan, 1896).

The Principles of Fruit-Growing (New York: Macmillan, 1897).

The Principles of Agriculture (New York: Macmillan, 1898).

Lessons with Plants: Suggestions for Seeing and Interpreting Some of the Common Forms of Vegetation (New York: Macmillan, 1898).

The Pruning-Book: A Monograph of the Pruning and Training of Plants as Applied to American Conditions (New York: Macmillan, 1898).

First Lessons with Plants: Being an Abridgement of "Lessons with Plants" (New York: Macmillan, 1898).

Garden-Making: Suggestions for Utilizing of Home Grounds (New York: Macmillan, 1898).

Sketch of the Evolution of Our Native Fruits (New York: Macmillan, 1898).

Botany: An Elementary Text for Schools (New York: Macmillan, 1900).

The Principles of Vegetable-Gardening (New York: Macmillan, 1901).

Nature Portraits: Studies with Pen and Camera of Our Wild Birds, Animals, Fish, and Insects (New York: Doubleday, Page & Co., 1902).

The Nature-Study Idea: Being an Interpretation of the New School-Movement to Put the Child in Sympathy with Nature (New York: Doubleday, Page & Co., 1903).

Outlook to Nature (New York: Macmillan, 1905).

The State and the Farmer (New York: Macmillan, 1908).

First Course in Biology, part 1, *Plant Biology* (New York: Macmillan, 1908) [parts 2 and 3 by W. M. Coleman].

Beginners Botany (New York: Macmillan, 1908).

Poems (Ithaca, NY: The Cornell Countryman, 1908).

The Training of Farmers (New York: The Century Co., 1909).

Manual of Gardening: A Practical Guide to the Making of Home Grounds and the Growing of Flowers, Fruits, and Vegetables for Home Use (New York: Macmillan, 1910).

The Country-life Movement in the United States (New York: Macmillan, 1911).

Farm and Garden Rule-Book: A Manual of Ready Rules and Reference with Recipes, Precepts, Formulas, and Tabular Information for Use of General Farmers, Gardeners, Fruit-Growers, Stockmen, Dairymen, Poultrymen, Foresters, Rural Teachers, and Others in the United States and Canada (New York: Macmillan, 1911) [previous edition published under the title *The Horticulturalist's Rule-Book*].

Outlook (Ithaca, NY: self-published, 1911).

Report of the Commission on Country Life (New York: Sturgis & Walton Co., 1911).

Botany for Secondary Schools: A Guide to the Knowledge of the Vegetation of the Neighborhood (New York: Macmillan, 1913) [previously published as *Botany: An Elementary Text for Schools*].

York State Rural Problems, vols. 1 and 2 (Albany: J.B. Lyon Co., 1913, 1915).

The Pruning-Manual (New York: Macmillan, 1916).

Ground Levels in Democracy (Ithaca, NY: self-published, 1916).

Wind and Weather (New York: Cornell Publishing Co., 1916) [collected poems].

The Holy Earth (Ithaca, NY: Comstock Publishing Co., 1918).

Home Grounds, Their Planning and Planting (Harrisburg, PA: American Association of Nurserymen, 1918).

What Is Democracy? (Ithaca, NY: Comstock Publishing Co., 1918).

Universal Service, the Hope of Humanity (New York: Sturgis & Walton, 1918).

The School-Book of Farming: A Text for the Elementary Schools, Homes, and Clubs (New York: Macmillan, 1920).

The Nursery-Manual: A Complete Guide to the Multiplication of Plants (New York: Macmillan, 1920).

The Apple Tree (New York: Macmillan, 1922).

The Cultivated Evergreens: A Handbook of the Coniferous and Most Important Broad-leaved Evergreens Planted for Ornament in the United States and Canada (New York: Macmillan, 1923).

The Seven Stars (New York: Macmillan, 1923).

Manual of Cultivated Plants: A Flora for the Identification of the Most Common or Significant Species of Plants Grown in the Continental United States and Canada, for Food, Ornament, Utility, and General Interest, Both in the Open and under Glass (New York: Macmillan, 1924).

The Gardener: A Book of Brief Directions for the Growing of the Common Fruits, Vegetables and Flowers in the Garden and about the House (New York: Macmillan, 1925).

The Harvest of the Year to the Tiller of the Soil (New York: Macmillan, 1927).

The Garden Lover (New York: Macmillan, 1928).

The Cultivated Conifers in North America, Comprising the Pine Family and the Taxads: Successor to "The Cultivated Evergreens" (New York: Macmillan, 1933).

How Plants Get Their Names (New York: Macmillan, 1933).

Gardener's Handbook, Successor to "The Gardener": Brief Indications for the Growing of Common Flowers, Vegetables and Fruits in the Garden and about the Home (New York: Macmillan, 1934).

The Garden of Gourds, with Decorations (New York: Macmillan, 1937).

The Garden of Pinks, with Decorations (New York: Macmillan, 1938).

The Garden of Larkspurs, with Decorations (New York: Macmillan, 1939).

Manual of Cultivated Plants Most Commonly Grown in the Continental United States and Canada (New York: Macmillan, 1949) [completely revised version of 1924 edition].

The Garden of Bellflowers in North America, with Decorations (New York: Macmillan, 1953).

BOOKS WRITTEN UNDER JOINT AUTHORSHIP

L. H. Bailey and E. Z. Hortus, *A Concise Dictionary of Gardening, General Horticulture and Cultivated Plants in North America* (New York: Macmillan, 1930).

————. *Supplement to Hortus, for the Five Current Years Including 1930* (New York: Macmillan, 1935).

————. *Hortus Second: A Concise Dictionary of Gardening, General Horticulture and Cultivated Plants in North America* (New York: Macmillan, 1941).

Charles E. Hunn and L. H. Bailey, *The Amateur's Practical Garden-Book; Containing the Simplest Directions for the Growing of the Commonest Things about the House and Garden* (New York: Macmillan, 1913).

Sites

Bailey and Eustace-Cole Hall, East Circle Drive, Michigan State University, East Lansing, Michigan

Liberty Hyde Bailey Museum, 903 Bailey Avenue, South Haven, Michigan 49090

Statue in Annual Trial Garden behind Plant and Soil Science Building, Bogue Street, Michigan State University, East Lansing, Michigan

Ringgold Wilmer Lardner

Life Is More Than a Game

March 6, 1885–September 25, 1933
Born in Niles

. . . .

To truly laugh, you must be able to take your pain and play with it.—CHARLIE CHAPLIN

If what used to be known as the national pastime had a poet laureate, his name was Ring Lardner. The first prominent writer to capture the singular language of the baseball world and its diamond-in-the-rough characters, Lardner won national fame and wealth—but at cost.

Evoking the earthy nature, tangled lexicon, and lowbrow philosophy of the baseball world in fictional works such as *You Know Me, Al,* Lardner was regarded as a first-rate satirist and humorist. Yet always beneath the laughter he inspired was a melancholy that suggested concealed depths and unspoken words. But he never surmounted his disappointment in the hypocrisy and self-delusions of his fellow citizens, even as he harnessed it to write classic American short stories.

A stagecoach stop on the Sauk Trail between Chicago and Detroit, Niles was settled in 1828 and named for publisher Hezekiel Niles. It developed as a center for the farm produce of the St. Joseph River valley, and also the site

Ring Lardner (seated in front) and his mother and siblings pose on the front porch of their Niles home. His beloved mother's scripted shows for the neighborhood children contributed to Ring's penchant for performance in writing and in life. Courtesy of Fort St. Joseph Museum.

of manufacturing that included paper products, industrial and assembly-line equipment, wire, and commercial refrigerators.

By most accounts, Ring's Niles childhood was one of material comfort, family warmth, and high spirits. Descended from a family that had become rooted in the community after arriving in 1836, the Lardners, during Ring's childhood, inhabited a large gray stucco house with gabled roofs on Bond Street, not far from the bank of the St. Joseph River. (Divided into apartments, the house still stands; a state historical marker tells Ring's story from across the street.) In addition to Ring, his parents, and siblings, the abode had room for several servants.

Allegedly 14 pounds at birth on March 6, 1885, and the youngest of his family (twelve years younger than his oldest sister), Ringgold Wilmer Lardner was gregarious from the start. Able to entertain townsfolk and aware of his talent, the young Ring was also the comic and cutup of the household, prone to practical jokes. While he respected his father, he adored his mother, a kind and doting woman who sketched out plays for the children of the

The Lardner family home in Niles, now divided into apartments, is recognized by a State of Michigan historical marker across the street. Critics have debated whether Ring Lardner's writing mocked the pretensions of the small-town America in which he grew up, or simply held its image up to the mirror for his Midwestern readers to enjoy and laugh at in recognition. Courtesy of Michigan Historic Preservation Office.

neighborhood. Ring was one of the primary actors after a time. His mother homeschooled him until he was twelve.

His career in high school was unremarkable but for two things: he graduated at age sixteen and wrote what is believed to be his first published work, the class poem, which appeared in the *Niles Daily Star* in June 1901.

Already deeply rooted in small-town America, baseball was a popular game in Niles. To Ring it also represented the larger world—and the same kind of glamour as the stage. Around the time of his high school graduation, he encountered Ed Reulbach, then a Notre Dame pitcher who came to Niles to play. Preparing for the game, Reulbach sat down on the team bench. "Suddenly a tin-cup full of water was offered. I glanced at the individual and almost fell off the bench," Reulbach remembered. "There was the same kid I saw at the Saturday game when he asked to be water boy. He sat next to me on the bench and offered me a cup of water every few minutes, until I finally told him that I did not need a bath, just a cup of water every other inning."

But not all in the young man's life was simplicity and sunshine. Ring was hobbled until the age of eleven, wearing a brace to correct what one biographer called "a deformed foot." And in 1901 the well-to-do family suffered a serious reversal. Ring's father, Henry, invested in a bank in Duluth, Minnesota, where his oldest son William had become a partner. The bank failed and so did other investments. The family wealth was almost depleted, and Ring's world changed.

The same year, after graduating, Ring moved to Chicago to pursue paying work. But he never got farther than office boy. Leaving two jobs, after two weeks each, with the mutual consent of his employers, Ring returned to Niles and quickly lost a third job, this time with the Michigan Central Railroad. His father then encouraged Ring and brother Rex to study engineering, and they proceeded to Chicago's Armour Institute in 1902. Ring flunked all of his subjects except rhetoric. Another return to Niles followed. After resting and time as a substitute mail carrier, he acquired a job in 1904 as bookkeeper for the Niles Gas Company at $5 a week, later boosted to $8.

During this time, Ring produced his first significant artistic creation. A member of the American Minstrels, a group of local young men who staged then-popular minstrel shows, Ring authored the music and tongue-in-cheek lyrics of a two-act musical dubbed *Zanzibar*. Staged in April 1903, the production was a community hit and made a small profit.

His first big break came in the autumn of 1905. For $12 a week he became a reporter for the *South Bend Times*, authoring a regular column of Niles news, among other assignments, and indulging his affection for baseball as both reporter and official scorer for the South Bend entry in the Central League. After Ring demonstrated his horsehide wisdom to editor Hugh Fullerton at the 1907 World Series, the older man referred him to a friend at the *Chicago Inter-Ocean*. Soon after, Fullerton recommended Ring for a job at the *Chicago Examiner*. In March 1909 he got the assignment to cover the Chicago White Sox. As much an extra member of the team as a reporter, Ring was a favorite of the players—and shared abundant liquid refreshments with them between games.

Ring had found his milieu and subject matter. Ring shaped the itinerant, semiliterate, and alternately cagey and oblivious athlete into art. In 1913, he obtained a daily column at the *Chicago Tribune*, "In the Wake of the News," and began fitting the natural patois of the baseballers into his fiction. The *Saturday Evening Post* published many of Ring's pieces, collected in 1916 in the volume *You Know Me Al: A Busher's Letters*. Authored by the fictional also-ran pitcher Jack Keefe, the letters struck many as not only hilarious in their depiction of a self-important, myopic, but basically decent American, but also as a rendering of authentic American speech caught in art. A sample:

FRIEND AL: Coming out of Amarillo last night I and Lord and Weaver was sitting at the dining table in the dining car with a old lady. None of us were talking to her but she looked me over pretty careful and seemed to kind of like my looks. Finally she says Are you boys with some football club. Lord nor Weaver didn't say anything so I thought it was up to me and I says no mam this is the Chicago White Sox Ball Club. She says I knew you were athaletes. I says Yes I guess you could spot us for athaletes. She says Yes indeed and specially you. You certainly look healthy. I says You ought to see me stripped. I didn't see nothing funny about that but I thought Lord and Weaver would die laughing. Lord had to get up and leave the table and he told everybody what I said.

The laughter rang hollow for Ring, however, when gamblers bribed eight members of the White Sox to throw the 1919 World Series. The game that had symbolized the pure and golden was now tainted by scandal. Disillusioned, and also seeking a larger and more lucrative forum for his talents, Ring left his job as *Tribune* variety columnist and sportswriter, moved east to New York to continue his fiction writing and pursue his hope of penning musicals, and settled his family in Great Neck, Long Island. That family included his wife Ellis (a native of Goshen, Indiana, whom he had married in 1911) and four sons. One of them—Ring, Jr.—would go on to fame of his own, winning Academy Awards for the screenplays of *Woman of the Year* and *M*A*S*H*.

The stories kept coming even as Ring struggled to find a venue for the musicals. His neighbor and fellow drinker in Great Neck, F. Scott Fitzgerald, found art as well as entertainment in Ring's fiction and convinced his publisher, Charles Scribner's Sons, to turn out a volume of what Fitzgerald regarded as Lardner's ten best stories. The collection, *How to Write Short Stories*, was a success. *The Love Nest and Other Stories* followed in 1926, containing the classic story "Haircut," whose first-person narrative mingles satirical humor and small-town darkness. Editor Maxwell Perkins wrote Ring to say, "I can't shake it out of my mind—in fact the impression it made has deepened with time. There's not a man alive who could have done better, that's for certain." Also in 1926, critic H. L. Mencken said of Ring's work: "He is trying to do something that no other current fictioneer has tried to do. Without wasting any wind on statements of highfalutin esthetic or ethical purpose, he is trying to get the low-down Americano between covers."[1]

But even as his fame and reputation grew, Ring was plagued by depression as well as alcoholism. The third stage of Ring's career—as a songwriter and lyricist—marked his final years. His only successful Broadway production was a collaboration with George S. Kaufman on *June Moon* in 1929. He continued to write for the stage, but tuberculosis joined his maladies and resulted in his early death in 1933 at the age of forty-eight.

In the decades since, Ring's reputation has risen and fallen. Alternately written off as a minor satirist and admired as an insightful portrayer of the Midwestern everyman, there is general agreement that Ring's style influenced such renowned artists as Ernest Hemingway and J. D. Salinger to write dialogue and interior monologue as they heard it, not as it was supposed to be.

It is in Ring's Niles roots that some of the controversy lies. Was he mocking the pretensions of small-town America in which he grew up, or holding its image up to the mirror for his Midwestern readers to enjoy and laugh at in recognition? While critics have often characterized his work as subtly ridiculing the soon-to-be-frustrated aspirations of middle-class Midwesterners, biographer Jonathan Yardley took a different view, saying the author "understood that it is the fate of most of us to struggle toward insubstantial goals and to fail even in that, and he was amused in a sad and pensive way by what he saw from that Olympian peak he occupied, but he watched with compassion rather than contempt, dismay rather than distaste."

Fitzgerald, who ultimately disparaged Ring for spending his talent on a boy's game, nonetheless left behind two haunting portraits of what is believed to be Ring: in *The Great Gatsby*, the minor character "Owl Eyes" (a name bestowed on him by the White Sox); and in *Tender Is the Night*, Abe North, tall like the six-foot-two Ring and possessed of his sad, deep-set eyes and the desire to be a songwriter.

More than Ring's childhood home remains in Niles. There is a Ring Lardner Middle School. And inscribed on the base of the organ that he pumped as a child in Trinity Episcopal Church are etched the initials "R.L." His name is also etched in the book of authentic American literature.

Works

• •

Bib Ballads (Chicago: P.F. Volland, 1915).

You Know Me Al: A Busher's Letters (New York : G.H. Doran, 1916).

Gullible's Travels and Other Stories (Indianapolis: Bobbs-Merrill, 1918).

Treat 'Em Rough: Letters from Jack the Kaiser Killer (Indianapolis: Bobbs-Merrill, 1918).

The Real Dope (Indianapolis: Bobbs-Merrill, 1919).

Own Your Own Home (Indianapolis: Bobbs-Merrill; Braunworth and Co., 1919).

The Young Immigrunts (Indianapolis: Bobbs-Merrill; Curtis Publishing Co., 1920).

The Big Town: How I and the Mrs. Go to New York to See Life and Get Katie a Husband (Indianapolis: Bobbs-Merrill, 1921).

Symptoms of Being 35 (Indianapolis: Bobbs-Merrill, 1921).

Say It with Oil: A Few Remarks about Wives (paired in the same book with Nina Wilcox Putnam's *Say it with Bricks*) (New York: George H. Doran Co., 1923).

How to Write Short Stories (New York: Charles Scribner's Sons, 1924).

What of It? (New York and London: Charles Scribner's Sons, 1925).

The Love Nest and Other Stories (New York: Charles Scribner's Sons, 1926).

The Story of a Wonder Man: Being the Autobiography of Ring Lardner (New York: Charles Scribner's Sons, 1927).

Round Up: The Stories of Ring W. Lardner (New York: Charles Scribner's Sons, 1929).

June Moon: A Comedy in a Prologue and Three Acts, with George S. Kaufman (New York: Charles Scribner's Sons, 1930).

Lose with a Smile (New York: Charles Scribner's Sons, 1933).

First and Last (New York, London: Charles Scribner's Sons, 1934).

Sites

• •

Childhood home, 519 Bond Street, Niles, Michigan

Ring Lardner Middle School, 801 N. 17th St., Niles, Michigan

Carl Sandburg

Sand Man

January 6, 1878–July 22, 1967
Lived in Tower Hill and Harbert

. . . .

Like legions of Chicagoans throughout the twentieth century, during the
summer of 1926 a middle-aged married couple journeyed south around the
bottom of Lake Michigan to rent a cottage. They found the right location
close to Tower Hill near the town of Sawyer, Michigan, just south of a pristine dune area. Overlooking the lake, the diminutive white house would
serve as a haven of rest and relaxation after an intense period of productive work for the husband. Both of Scandinavian descent, the couple also
enjoyed their proximity via the Red Arrow Highway to Harbert, a small
village blessed with an exquisite Swedish bakery. Their primary purpose,
though, was the freshwater shoreline experience. It was like reliving their
first days together.

Years before, as a young community organizer, Carl Sandburg had
courted a young schoolteacher and Phi Beta Kappa graduate of the
University of Chicago named Lilian Steichen, while rounding up support
from Wisconsinites for political change. While missing the woman he

endearingly nicknamed "Paula," he walked the Lake Michigan shoreline near Two Rivers. In a typically effusive letter, he wrote her:

> Just had a 5-mile hike—over sandy hills wild and wind beaten, and into pine woods along the lake shore. I looked up at the sky and startlingly near, through the green-black boughs of a massive pine, I saw a glowing star, a glittering, melting, concentrated flame seen through this one hole in the roof of the forest . . . And so good night, my great heart, like the pines and stars I worshipped with tonight—good night. I kiss your grand face. It is a night of grandeurs—and you are its star. I kiss you as the last glory of this night of glories.

After their wedding, Milwaukee became the couple's home. Its proximity to Lake Michigan enabled them to pay frequent visits to the water's edge, to see more of those glowing stars. Paula had been born in Upper Peninsula's Hancock, and she was no stranger to water. The lake that bore her home state's name was a frequent companion during the couple's first days together.

Earnings from his successful biography of fellow Illinoisan Abraham Lincoln, published just before settling into Tower Hill, gave the Sandburgs financial freedom that years of writing poetry had not achieved. Verse had won him acclaim, a regular job at the *Chicago Daily News*, and an invitation to author the seminal biography, but Carl had not realized how much would be involved in researching, outlining, and authoring *The Prairie Years*— the first half of an intended complete Lincoln study—especially given the unconventional approach he employed. Unfootnoted, full of soaring poetic passages, the two-volume work met with general critical acclaim but not a full embrace by professional historians. "For thirty years and more I have planned to make a certain portrait" of Lincoln, Sandburg wrote in the preface, his efforts to be of service well beyond history, to "poetry, art, human behavior." Now that he was halfway through the daunting project, he was faced with additional burdensome assignments for the newspaper. The first summer at the Michigan beachfront was a happy but short interlude before returning to duty in Chicago.

Next on the writing agenda was a compilation of traditional folk-music pieces—what he would call *American Songbag*—requiring the enormous labor of sifting through thousands of tunes and stories, learning how to play them on his guitar until he caught their key, assimilating and adjudging, writing

Carl Sandburg on the Lake Michigan bluff at Harbert. Nearby, he and spouse Lilian Steichen built a house with an upper writing studio where he could draw inspiration from waves and wind. Used with permission of the Rare Book & Manuscript Library of the University of Illinois at Urbana–Champaign and Carl Sandburg Family Trust.

commentary, laying it aside for other work. Many requests came in. When Sandburg was on a sightseeing trip to Thomas Jefferson's home at Monticello in April 1927, the editor at the *University of Virginia Quarterly* asked the favor of receiving some poems to publish. A children's book was on the drawing board. A book-length poem entitled *Good Morning America* was beginning to take shape. The *Chicago Daily News* still required regular columns and news-based reporting. Speaking engagements on behalf of *The Prairie Years* and his poetry carried him across the country. A lot was left to be done, most notably the remaining account of Lincoln and the American Civil War.

By the summer of 1927, life in the husky, brawling City of the Big Shoulders had worn him out. Nearly fifty and no longer able to expend himself as youth had once permitted, Carl suffered an emotional collapse. With her husband bedridden, Paula decided there was one tonic: to buy the Tower Hill house they had enjoyed so much the previous year and spend more time there. So, the family packed up, again made the trip through Indiana to Sawyer, and settled into the little white house, renaming it "Wren Cottage."

To facilitate Carl's recovery and nurture his muse, the Sandburgs built a studio separate from the main structure in which he could work when able. In the meantime, the watchword for the rest of the family—all female—was to be quiet. The guitar hung on the wall of the studio, silent. Uncurtained windows enabled tranquil views "amid the sand hills of Michigan" into what they hoped would be a restorative Nature. One poem written here upon their arrival, *Bundles*, exemplifies Carl's state of exhaustion:

I have thought of beaches, fields,
Tears, laughter.

I have thought of homes put up—And blown away.

I have thought of meetings and for
Every meeting a good-by.

I have thought of stars going alone,
Orioles in pairs, sunsets in blundering
Wistful deaths.

I have wanted to let go and cross over
To a next star, a last star.

I have asked to be left a few tears
And some laughter.

In another, fraying is evident as he rails, "Shut the windows, open the doors. There are no windows, are no doors?" Within weeks, though, the waves, the sky, the grasses were soothing his overwrought mind. Carl's outlook became more positive, as conveyed by these later words, a mirror contrast: "You shall have peace; the mist creeps, the doors open. Let night, let sleep, have their way."

For many Michigan residents and visitors, summer memories are intertwined with cottages on lakes, serene moments spent in lawn chairs overlooking the water. Well-trodden paths down to a lake illustrate the magnetism of water. As the sun luxuriously made its way up and over the cottage to sink at day's end into the horizon over Illinois, the Sandburg family grew closer, stronger, fresher. Under the summer moon, the water shimmered

A senior Sandburg and grandson on the leeward side of his beloved Lake Michigan. Used with permission of the Rare Book & Manuscript Library of the University of Illinois at Urbana–Champaign and Carl Sandburg Family Trust.

as it had for generations, reaching back to the Natives who had come long before. Majestic Lake Michigan and its sweet sand fringe became more than an escape; they became home. Year-round.

Although Big Blue began to restore him, the Sandburgs found that fame was difficult to escape. No real boundary separated Tower Hill from the adjacent Warren Dunes State Park; inquisitive campers and day visitors frequently interrupted the solitude of the poet's retreat. But the Sandburgs had no intention of abandoning the Michigan lakeshore and began looking for other nearby property. They soon found it down the beach in Harbert, much closer to the community of Norsemen and the bakery that had first made the Sandburgs feel so at home. In 1928, they purchased land from the developer of a resort to be known as "Birchwood Beach." Paula designed a three-story manor house that faced the lake, situated on a pine-studded bluff to take advantage of the vistas, generously supplied with windows all around, and topped with a crow's nest reached via seventeen steps to a roof deck. The house was of Dutch Colonial design with several dormers, complementary end fireplaces, a conservatory, shingled roof, and nearby shed. The private road out front came to be known, appropriately, as Poets Path; they referred to the beach home as Chikaming Farm, after the Native American name given to the township. Carl first called it "Paw Paw Farm," after the native tree and its characteristic fruit found in abundance nearby.

Assembled from seven lots over five acres, the property became the Sandburgs' home for the next two decades. When necessary, Carl took the train from Harbert into Chicago, but this practice soon became infrequent. Instead, the third floor of the house, which he made into a writing studio, became his escape. On especially nice days, Carl would take his typewriter, notes, and green eyeshade onto the west-facing deck outside the office, where—ever more tanned in contrast to his white shock of hair—he would write, write, write. Rejuvenated, with a new lease on life, he began to shape the remainder of the Lincoln biography. *The Prairie Years* comprised two volumes; he would end up doubling that output over the next dozen years as he labored to tell the story of how Abe Lincoln saved the Union.

The Sandburgs loved Harbor Country, through all the seasons. "It is an odd corner of the world, a slow sickle of beach curving 22 miles to the headland where at night we see the pier lights of Benton Harbor—and in winter the splinters of the Northern Lights. Across the lake to the west we see the half-circle moving white spike of the Lindbergh beacon in Chicago. The lake performs. The lake runs a gamut of all moods." Thus did Carl sum up the view from his beach house. Odd, and immensely satisfactory. And inspirational.

Although Lincoln was the centerpiece of the next two decades of work, Sandburg often wrote about the inland "sea" named after the state he had made his residence. One piece contained this evocative beginning:

On the shores of Lake Michigan
high on a wooden pole, in a box,
two purple martins had a home
and taken away down to Martinique
and let loose, they flew home,
thousands of miles to be home again.
    And this has lights of wonder
echo and pace and echo again.[1]

Scenes on the beach inspired a number of poems, including *Broken Sky*:

> The sky of gray is eaten in six places,
> Rag holes stand out,
> It is an army blanket and the sleeper
> slept too near the fire.

Perhaps the most beautiful work is *Lake Michigan Morning*:

> Blue and white came out,
> Riders of an early fall morning,
> The blue by itself, the white by itself.
>
> A young lamb white
> crossed on a clear water blue.
> Blue rollers talked on a beach white sand.
> Water blown from snowwhite mountains
> met the blue rise of lowland waters.
> This was an early morning of high price.
> Blue bowls of white water
> Poured themselves into white bowls of blue water.
> There was a back-and-forth and a kiss-me kill-me
> washing and weaving.

In eight verses entitled *Little Sketch*, the famed poet led the reader gently into the evening light he had come to love:

> There are forked branches of trees
> Where the leaves shudder obediently,
> Where the hangover leaves
> Flow in a curve downward;
> And between the forks and leaves,
> In patches and angles, in square handfuls,
> The orange lights of the done sunset
> Come and filter and pour.

Carl enjoyed reading this poetry at homes along the beachfront; his voice made the poems come to life for his neighbors. He would walk the dunes for inspiration, take his grandson down to water's edge to play and skip stones, revel in the westerly wind and ever-present waves. The family would go boating on the big lake, swim in its refreshing waters, and comb its shore for driftwood and detritus. His recreational pursuits even extended to golf at nearby Bridgman. Carl Sandburg had found a place that saved his career—and, perhaps, his life.

It had been a lifelong ambition to write of his fellow Prairie Stater, and Sandburg tackled the second half of the Lincoln life story with renewed energy. Often working late into the night, with the third-story window open to the waves lapping or crashing, he sifted through notes, photos, books, sources on Lincoln, relying on the help of his three daughters as research aides. In the morning, knowing he had labored late, they would leave him breakfast and coffee outside the office for when he awakened. The garret made the perfect perch, lined with filing cabinets packed with notes and documents, featuring a cot and stove, and lit as darkness arrived by a dual florescent light. In keeping with beachfront informality, he used a crate for a desk. When challenged on this novel setup, Sandburg replied, "If General Grant could command his troops from an old crate, I can certainly write about it from one." He spent a dozen years crafting the remaining four volumes in the series entitled *Abraham Lincoln: The War Years*, and its reception was appropriate. In 1940, Sandburg won the Pulitzer Prize for his Michigan-written epic examination of the wartime president—this time with its million-and-a-half words fully referenced.

While her husband and children were working together upstairs, Paula was engaged in managing the household, gardening, and raising livestock. When first married, and while Carl earned but a meager living, the resourceful Paula supplemented their stores by raising chickens. In the summer of 1935 she purchased three goats for Chikaming Farm, disappointing daughter Helga's wish for a cow. It became a life-altering decision for the family. The shed in front became "Tom Thumb Dairy" as Paula and Helga carried goat raising to an expert level. In 1940, the Pulitzer year, Paula's goats won their own awards and set records for milk production. Within a decade, the flock of three had grown to over two hundred prizewinners valued for their breeding and production.

Thus it was that the foreword to the second Lincoln series, dated July 1939, originated from "Chikaming Goat Farm Harbert, Michigan." Included in the massive number of credits were several folks from Harbert, including a "Lake Michigan shoreline neighbor." After so many fruitful years on that shoreline, his task was finally over; the last sentence was penned, recording Lincoln's interment: "The prairie years, the war years, were over." When a collection of three verse works was published in 1941, Sandburg wrote the preface and dated it "September 30" from the same location: "Chikaming Goat Farm Harbert, Michigan." The address remained the same through the Second World War.

Toward the end of 1945, the teeming goat herd forced the Sandburgs to leave Michigan for bigger and more year-round pastures. With Paula's expertise in goat raising still to be fully exploited, the family relocated to Flat Rock, North Carolina, on an expansive estate named Connemara. It would become a national landmark. Two railroad boxcars were needed to empty the Chikaming farmhouse of papers. Carl added to that legacy with some more writing at Connemara, but he was in his late sixties with the bulk of his career behind him. It was the work in Michigan that had confirmed his fame.

When he passed away in the summer of 1967, a half century after breaking into the nation's consciousness with his first Pulitzer winner, it was his wish to be buried back in the Midwest, at Galesburg, his childhood home. Carl Sandburg—most Americans knew the name as one of the nation's largest literary figures. Without two decades of fruitful labor on the West Michigan shore, the Sandburg legacy might never have become so rich. He recognized as much before departing for the South in 1945, making a final, brief appearance at a New Year's Eve party, where he was unable to utter a word to his Harbert neighbors as tears filled his eyes. As departure from the Michigan Riviera loomed, he uttered a melancholy lament to a fellow reporter in what sounds like the concluding verse to a poem, a coda to the music of the lake he had listened to every night for nearly two decades:

"I love it here. I love to skip stones.
I'm going to miss it all."

Works

You and Your Job (Chicago: Charles H. Kerr & Co., 1908).

Abraham Lincoln: The Prairie Years (New York: Harcourt Brace and Co., 1926).

The American Songbag (New York: Harcourt Brace and Co., 1927).

Mary Lincoln: Wife and Widow (New York: Harcourt Brace and Co., 1932).

Abraham Lincoln: The War Years (New York: Harcourt Brace and Co., 1939).

Storm over the Land (New York: Harcourt Brace and Co., 1942).

Home Front Memo (New York: Harcourt Brace and Co., 1943).

Remembrance Rock (New York: Harcourt Brace and Co., 1948).

Lincoln Collector (New York: Harcourt Brace and Co., 1949).

The New American Songbag (New York: Broadcast Music, Inc., 1950).

Always the Young Strangers (New York: Harcourt Brace and Co., 1953).

A Lincoln Preface (New York: Harcourt Brace and Co., 1953).

Abraham Lincoln: The Prairie Years and the War Years (New York: Harcourt Brace and Co., 1954).

Sites

Lake Michigan shoreline near Harbert, between Lakeside, Michigan, and Sawyer, Michigan

The Harbert Swedish Bakery and Luisa's Cafe, 13689 Red Arrow Highway, Harbert, Michigan 49115

Tower Hill cottage, Tower Hill Road, Sawyer, Michigan

Northern Lower Michigan

Charles Bruce Catton

America's Civil War Storyteller

October 9, 1899–August 28, 1978

Born in Petoskey; grew up in Benzonia; graduate of Benzonia Academy; longtime resident of Frankfort

"The Civil War is, for the American imagination, the great single event of our history." So wrote Pulitzer Prize–winner Robert Penn Warren. For generation after generation of Civil War readers, Michigan's Bruce Catton is the single greatest writer to ever make that history come alive. Unlike many history books that are not widely known or do not survive much beyond the authors' own lifetimes, Catton's classics continue to be published, read, and enjoyed, then passed on to the next generation.

Bruce Catton had no formal training as a historian. By profession a journalist, he wrote for newspapers much of his adult life, and served during World War II in public relations as director of information for the U.S. War Production Board. The latter experience led him to write his first book, on the subject of wartime Washington. Though not a commercial success, its publication opened a new vista as he approached his fiftieth birthday. Catton had been in the nation's capital during historic times, serving his country as a civilian during the world's worst conflict. This experience helped lead him into devoting his writing abilities to a previous era of

Charles Bruce Catton, full of midlife
vigor, early in the era when he became
the nation's premier Civil War historian.
During a northern Michigan childhood,
he was enthralled by local veterans'
reminiscences, which inspired his
writing. Courtesy of the Benzie Area
Historical Museum.

America in conflict, one that he had first encountered as a boy growing up in Michigan.

Catton turned to the full-time writing of history with a focus on the American Civil War. He published the first of a three-volume study on the Union Army of the Potomac in 1951, a time when a war-weary public did not form a very receptive audience. The trilogy's opening volume was a modest success, as was the middle issue of the series. Within a couple of years came the concluding work—and the astonishing award of a Pulitzer Prize in history for *A Stillness at Appomattox*. In just a few years, Catton would be chosen to write the seminal history of the War during the Civil War Centennial, 1961 to 1965. No other option existed.

How a middle-aged newspaperman became the premier and enduring Civil War historian is a story made possible only by the writer's boyhood in northwestern lower Michigan. Few places in the state are tinier than Benzonia, and few exceed the beauty of its setting. Situated on the rise of a hill just a walk from aptly named Crystal Lake, the village remains similar to when it was founded on the cusp of the Civil War. Its origin was influenced by the biblical metaphor of a "city on a hill" that would serve as a beacon of light to the community's residents. As Catton grew up, he grew to know veterans, the pillars of the village, who had marched away decades before his birth to the great task of saving the nation. A place with vision and its humble people gave Catton inspiration for his ultimate success.

After the 1899 birth of their oldest boy in the lakeside resort town of Petoskey, Catton's parents had moved the family south to Benzonia so that his father could serve as instructor and headmaster of the town academy, a Christian college preparatory school. As Catton would later recount, the settlement was likely the only one for miles around without lumbering as its main reason for existence. Faith, family, and community nurtured his youth. Every Memorial Day and Fourth of July, the entire village would turn out to celebrate its American heritage with a patriotic parade in which gray-haired and long-bearded oldsters in faded blue outfits—and an occasional empty sleeve—stepped in a familiar though now shuffling cadence. Young Catton stared wide-eyed at these Civil War vets, the images of their youthful appearance on battlegrounds all over the country forever burned into his memory. The festivities always concluded with a modest ceremony in the hilltop village cemetery, flowers strewn across the graves, and the veterans wearing a faraway look as they remembered scenes and soldiers of that bygone era. Bygone, but, for the boy, so very real and true.

In the early part of the twentieth century, before the age of superhighways made possible by a world-dominant auto industry at the other end of the Lower Peninsula, rail served as the primary means of transport throughout Michigan. A depot appropriate to its small-town character was Benzonia's connection to the world at large. Young Catton watched many trains depart for destinations beyond the few streets of his little town. As an old man, he would write of a restlessness he felt then:

> Early youth is a baffling time. The present moment is nice but it does not last. Living in it is like waiting in a junction town for the morning limited; the junction may be interesting but some day you will have to leave it and you do not know where the limited will take you. Benzonia was a good place to wait for the morning train.

Raised in a religious family on the King James Bible, Catton developed a way with words at an early age. His father's preparatory academy served

The Benzonia Academy building, now the Mills Community House, where the Cattons lived and the future Pulitzer winner began seriously to write. A state historical marker commemorates the site. Photo by Jack Dempsey.

him well; at the age of sixteen, his abilities gained him the opportunity for higher education in nearby Ohio. Located near Cleveland, Oberlin College was another religious institution established by Christians seeking to create a community of scholars in a spiritual setting. College representatives had founded Benzonia. The school was affected by the prime cause of the Civil War, the struggle over slavery, and African Americans were granted admission in the 1830s. The college board of trustees included the father of abolitionist John Brown. Catton's decision to attend Oberlin linked him to a tradition that wove its way back to the antebellum era; these college years helped to permanently impress the War's legacy on the young man.

For a time, after leaving Oberlin early—restless again—Catton took up writing for newspapers in Cleveland. He served for two years in the U.S. Navy during World War I. Marriage followed, in 1925, to Hazel Cherry; fatherhood followed in 1926 with the birth of his only child. Catton's newspaper reporting had a certain grace to it and opened the door for a column, soon syndicated. Day after day he honed his craft, finding a way to appeal to the earnest sensibilities of Midwestern readers. This experience helped his writing to find its fullest expression nearly three decades later in *A Stillness*.

In 1954, the same year that the Pulitzer arrived, New York City came calling. The American Association for State and Local History bravely issued a quarterly but failing publication under the *American Heritage* banner. Several notable historians thought the struggling periodical deserved a wider readership, employing a more creative fashion and format. A hardcover magazine under that title soon debuted, and *American Heritage* became the most popular history publication in the United States. Catton's role as chief editor provided a major force for its success. In 1954 he was one of four founders of the newly styled periodical, also serving as a writer and reviewer. The first issue revealed his vision for the magazine:

> We intend to deal with that great, unfinished, and illogically inspiring story of the American people doing and being and becoming. Our American heritage is greater than any one of us. It can express itself in very homely truths; in the end it can lift up our eyes beyond the glow in the sunset skies.

Catton served for a quarter century as one of the principal editors; the publication continued listing him first on its masthead under "Former Editors" and lured potential subscribers with: "Experience the American Heritage Tradition of Excellence . . . Nearly 60 Years of Brilliant Writing." Catton is also listed among its "Respected Authors."

That quarter century of service would have been career enough for even a younger man. Catton, though, had much more to say besides writing columns and editing the work of others at the magazine. He continued on a parallel path of research and writing, publishing eleven more Civil War books. One of them was *Banners at Shenandoah*, a 1955 novel for young people whose hero hailed from a Michigan home not far from Lake Michigan. The little book presaged an even more popular work five years later.

Catton was the only conceivable candidate to pen the narrative for *The American Heritage Picture History of the Civil War*, published in 1960. Of all his works, this illustrated volume may be his greatest legacy. Heirloom dogeared copies on numerous home bookshelves of countless baby boomers and their progeny prove its lasting power. Catton's prose in both the full-length volume and the slimmer Golden Book edition dovetailed perfectly with extensive drawings, photos, and maps to capture young imaginations. It won a special Pulitzer citation in 1961.

After the premature death of historian Lloyd Lewis threatened a planned series on General U.S. Grant, Catton's fame prompted Lewis's widow to request his services in completing her husband's labor of love. Ever the Midwestern gentleman, Catton acceded and produced remaining volumes in 1960 and 1968 to further acclaim. A gentleman, yes, but Catton did not shy from direct assaults on mythmakers. True to his roots in the antislavery Old Northwest Territory, and with a firm sense of historical integrity, he had challenged the "Lost Cause" mythology so rampant in the War literature. Catton took on the notions that the South had not fought the War because of slavery and had lost solely due to its inferior resources. *This Hallowed Ground* was issued in 1956, in the early stages of the modern civil rights movement. Subtitled *The Story of the Union Side of the Civil War*, the book fired salvos at prevailing concepts. By the time the 100-year anniversary of the War rolled around, Catton had become the natural choice to task with writing the official Centennial history, given the rectitude of his convictions on the War's origins and meaning.

More books have been written about the Civil War than any other American historical period, and it is a solid measure of greatness to be regarded as the quintessential historian of the conflict. Catton went beyond names and dates to treat history as great storytelling. It may take but a single encounter with his writing—say, a passage on the War's end in *This Hallowed Ground*—to captivate a reader:

> Ended; yet, in a haunting way, forever unended. It had laid down an infinity of loss and grief on the land; it had created a shadowed purple twilight streaked with undying fire which would live on, deep in the mind and heart of the nation, as long as any memory of the past retained meaning. Whatever the American people might hereafter do would in one way or another take form and color from this experience. Under every dream and under every doubt there would be the tragic knowledge bought by this war, the awareness that triumph and disaster were the two aspects of something lying beyond victory, the remembrance of heartbreak

and suffering, and the moment of vision bought by people who had bargained for no vision but simply wanted to live at peace.[1]

Gentleman: a word not so much in vogue anymore, it aptly fit Bruce Catton. One of his coeditors described him as "courtly." A Pulitzer did not inflate his ego; it made him even more self-effacing. As subsequent editions increased his fame and fortune, Catton's humility deepened even more. He suffered with ineffable grace the mediocre writing of others that his editing skill rescued; he accepted with equanimity accolades from colleagues who marveled at a work ethic they struggled to match. Underlying that ethic was the foundation set long before as a boy in Benzonia: "I began to see, dimly, that what you do is set up your ideal of the man you wish you were, and act as if you really were that sort of man—and maybe, in the end, it comes true for you."[2]

Beyond the books came articles, reviews, prefaces for others' books, lectures, appearances at Civil War roundtables, and, most awkward, acceptance speeches. This last duty became a regular burden. Then came the National Book Award. An award, in his name, for lifetime achievement from the Society of American Historians. Over two dozen honorary degrees, from institutions such as Harvard and the University of Maryland and, ironically, Oberlin. The Presidential Medal of Freedom, the nation's highest civilian commendation, was awarded to Catton: "Man of letters, preeminent historian of the War Between the States, he made us hear the sounds of battle and cherish peace. He made us see the bleeding wound of slavery and hold man's freedom dear." The awards paid recognition to the storyteller; they also served as commendations that this writer of military history equally portrayed war's glory and horror.

At fifty, already a grandfatherly looking man, Catton left powerful impressions on coworkers and colleagues. They revered him. David McCullough, also a Pulitzer-quality historian, was among those who felt his influence. Catton's vision for the future had a wisdom befitting someone whose youth was rooted in an optimism about continual progress in the human condition. So he would say:

The fabric of American life is a seamless web. Everything fits in somewhere. History is a continuous process; it extends far back into the past, and it will go on—in spite of today's uneasy qualms—far into the future . . . History after all is the story of people: . . . the ordinary folk of America . . . have done and thought and dreamed some rather extraordinary things.

A Stillness changed his life and elevated him to fame. But Catton refused to completely trade small-town Michigan for the enticements of the Big Apple. In New York, he loved a corner table at the famed Algonquin Hotel, where writers and bons vivants had gathered for years to dazzle each other with wit, insight, and general conversation. But he also loved angling. Catton luxuriated in the solitude of rowing to one of his favorite spots, throwing out the anchor and then the line, and resting in the embrace of natural Michigan. Whether or not the excursion produced a catch was relatively unimportant. The point was simply to realize again that a man's life fit within a greater, unfolding story.

Beginning in 1959, Catton spent each summer away from city heat back in his childhood venue, returning in the fall to the *American Heritage* office with a manuscript for yet another Civil War work. A cottage home near Frankfort on Glory Road—the title of the second volume of his Army trilogy, as well as a testament to his upbringing—became a sanctuary during those wonderful summers, a place to read and write and refresh himself. It was located beyond the south shore of Crystal Lake, "a noble body of water" that "when the sun is out its color is a breath-taking, incredible, picture-postcard blue."[3] Manhattan might have become his office location, but something about his native countryside kept calling him back:

> There was always a soft green twilight in our woods; it was dim, even in the middle of the day, yet everything seemed to glow as if there was really plenty of light, only it was a little different from ordinary sunlight. It was always cool, and when you'd come to a stream it'd be clear as crystal, with cold water running over sand and pebbles and dead logs, and big trout lazying away in the pools or sliding up and down the riffles. I used to think those woods were about as much like heaven as anything I was ever likely to see.[4]

One professional reviewer understood: "If he loved the values of the old Midwest, he held a special fondness for his home state of Michigan. He still preferred the small towns of his boyhood."

As the passage of time brought his own story closer to its end, Catton had two final, lasting contributions to make in service to his home state. During the national Bicentennial, a publisher planned to issue a book for each of the states, authored by a native son or daughter whose style and perspective could produce an enduring work. Just as he had been called upon to be the official Civil War Centennial historian, Catton became the obvious choice for the Michigan volume in the series. The slim hardcover volume described Michigan better than any other book had done. He wrote of Michigan's past, but also of its "incalculable future, attractive and terrifying by turns." The subject was as challenging in its attempt to peer into that future as in its recounting of Michigan's thousand years of human habitation. It would inspire him to close out his career in an elegiac book.

Writing a memoir, Catton determined not to write an autobiography. That required an ego he could not assert. Rather, *Waiting for the Morning Train* fashioned a reminiscence full of the warmth and light of the small-town Michigan he had known and loved and that had lured him back. The book did not shy from dealing with change. It described how a childhood of innocence had crashed into World Wars I and II and the nuclear age, proving that humanity did not inexorably progress to a greater, more perfect community. *Waiting for the Morning Train* also recounted the memory of Grand Army of the Republic veterans he had imitated in play in the Benzonia park, "set apart" by their Civil War experiences in the great cause of preserving the Union. They were his connection to the great men he had written so well about: Grant, Sherman, Sheridan, Custer. As the years rolled on, the men in blue had quietly faded away: "One by one the old men went up to that sun-swept hilltop to sleep beneath the lilacs, and as they departed we began to lose more than we knew we were losing."

Toward the end of summer in 1978, Bruce Catton made his own final trip to that hilltop. He had one last look at the mirrored lake, one final view of "the limitless blue plain of Lake Michigan."[5] In the Benzonia Township Cemetery, on a hill southeast of town near Love Road, one can find an unassuming grave befitting the name on the headstone, nestled under the dappled shade cast by oaks and evergreens planted when he was a boy. The visitor is reminded of those days in Catton's youth when the town would march together to honor the memory of their townsmen who had served and saved their country. Now, Bruce Catton has crossed over the river and rests under the shade of the trees.

Decades after his passing, many of Catton's history books remain in print. His first trilogy was reissued as *Bruce Catton's Civil War*; no greater honor can be awarded a historian, living or deceased, than to be synonymous with his or her subject. Those who open up his books or articles discover, in memorable prose that is almost poetry, a bygone era of glory and tragedy that Catton's writing makes ever relevant. From coastal cities to central plains, from New England village to North Dakota farm, no writer has had more impact on the minds and hearts of Americans drawn to their heritage. Catton's lyrical writing remains essential to comprehending our storied and blood-baptized past.

And it all began, and ended, in Michigan.

Works

Warlords of Washington (New York: Harcourt Brace and Co., 1948).

Mr. Lincoln's Army (Garden City, NY: Doubleday, 1951; New York: Anchor Books, 1990) [Army of the Potomac Trilogy].

Glory Road (Garden City, NY: Doubleday, 1952; New York: Anchor Books, 1990).

A Stillness at Appomattox (Garden City, NY: Doubleday, 1953; New York: Anchor Books, 1990; Austin, TX: Holt, Rinehart and Winston, 2000).

U.S. Grant and the American Military Tradition (Boston: Little, Brown and Co., 1954).

Banners at Shenandoah: A Story of Sheridan's Fighting Cavalry (Garden City, NY: Doubleday, 1955).

This Hallowed Ground: The Story of the Union Side of the Civil War (Garden City, NY: Doubleday, 1956; Hertfordshire, England: Wordsworth Editions, 1998).

America Goes to War (Middletown, CT: Wesleyan University Press, 1958; New York: MJF Books, 1992).

The American Heritage Picture History of the Civil War (New York: American Heritage, 1960).

The Golden Book of the Civil War (New York: Golden Press, 1960).

Grant Moves South (Boston: Little, Brown and Co., 1960).

Michigan's Past and the Nation's Future (Detroit: Wayne State University Press, 1960).

The Meaning of the Civil War (Chicago: Chicago Historical Society, 1961).

The Coming Fury (Garden City, NY: Doubleday, 1961) [Centennial History of the Civil War].

Terrible Swift Sword (Garden City, NY: Doubleday, 1963).

Two Roads to Sumter (New York: McGraw-Hill, 1963) [with William Catton].

The Battle of Gettysburg (New York: American Heritage, 1963).

Mr. Lincoln's Army (New York: Pocket Books, 1964).

The Penguin Book of the American Civil War (Harmondsworth, England: Penguin Books, 1966).

Never Call Retreat (Garden City, NY: Doubleday, 1965).

Grant Takes Command (Boston: Little, Brown and Co., 1968, 1969).

The War Lords of Washington (New York: Greenwood Press, 1969).

The Inescapable Challenge Lincoln Left Us (Springfield, IL: Abraham Lincoln Association, 1970).

Prefaces to History (Garden City, NY: Doubleday, 1970).

The Civil War (New York: American Heritage, 1971; Boston: Houghton Mifflin, 2005).

Waiting for the Morning Train (Garden City, NY: Doubleday, 1972; Detroit: Wayne State University Press, 1987).

Gettysburg: The Final Fury (Garden City, NY: Doubleday, 1974; Norwalk, CT: Easton Press, 1974).

Michigan: A Bicentennial History (New York: W.W. Norton, 1976).

The Bold and Magnificent Dream: America's Founding Years, 1492–1815 (Garden City, NY: Doubleday, 1978).

Bruce Catton's America: Selections from His Greatest Works (New York: American Heritage, 1979).

Civil War (New York: Fairfax Press, 1980; New York: American Heritage, 1985).

Bruce Catton's Civil War (New York: Fairfax Press, 1984).

Reflections on the Civil War (Garden City, NY: Doubleday, 1981; Norwalk, CT: Easton Press, 1981; New York: Berkley Books, 1994.

Sites

Benzonia Township Cemetery, 8063 Love Road, Benzonia, Michigan
Crystal Lake Glory Road, Frankfort, Michigan
Mills Community House, 891 Michigan Avenue US-31, Benzonia, Michigan
Village of Benzonia, Michigan

Sara Gwendolyn Frostic

Spirit Indomitable

April 26, 1906–April 25, 2001
Born in Sandusky; lived in Croswell; grew up in Wyandotte; graduate of Theodore Roosevelt High School
in Wyandotte; attended Western State Normal School; longtime resident of Benzonia

Michigan has long been a boom state. Lumber, copper, autos, and more
have powered its economy, then sputtered or died. Times have been the
worst, and they have been the best, and they have been the worst again.
Dickens could feel at home here.

Boom times raise up a crop of overconfidence that storm clouds are far
off and that moth and locust will never return. Whenever Michiganders
fall into this complacency, a cyclone will appear suddenly and tear down
the house; then they lament a cruel fate. It takes a while to begin thinking
again about whether and how to rebuild, how to renew, how to go on. First,
they must ask: Is it even possible?

In Sandusky, a small community in Michigan's Thumb, Sara Gwendolyn
Frostic was born on April 26, 1906, the second of nine children for parents
Fred and Sara. It seemed an idyllic setting in the Saginaw Valley, where a
trip to nearby Lake Huron revealed a limitless horizon. Fred was a schoolmaster; Sara kept house, and with a firm hand. Kids had chores, for

Sara Gwendolyn Frostic in the act of creativity–characteristically outdoors. Courtesy of Gwen Frostic Prints LLC.

work was necessary for survival. It was the early twentieth century in this farming community, without many of the advances and resources that had come to the city. No matter. Life, though harsh, was good.

Then, life intruded. While she was still a toddler, a raging fever left little Gwen near death. She narrowly survived, but her parents discovered that the illness had marked her indelibly. Some form of palsy left her no longer a physically robust child. Gwen could not run, could not jump, could not engage in the normal activities of a child any longer. She could no longer keep up and was in danger of being left behind. The disability might well curtail whatever promise her life held.

When Gwen was twelve, her father became school superintendent in Wyandotte, a community downriver from Detroit. Fred Frostic was a person with many interests. A graduate of Michigan Normal College (today's Eastern Michigan University), he was keenly interested in Michigan nature;

The Victorian-style Frostic family home in Wyandotte, where Frostic's creativity first began to flourish. Photo by Jack Dempsey.

in geology, plants, photography, woodcarving, art, and furniture making; and in music. Fred led a community effort to enhance Wyandotte's schools through an ambitious construction program that featured beautiful design and architecture; functionalism was not enough. Sara, who had a teaching certificate from Michigan Normal, also had a creative side. She helped found a garden club in Wyandotte, and in their Downriver house Gwen was given a kitchen drawer full of supplies to make her own drawings. It gave her great joy.

The communities in the Thumb could not have been more different from Wyandotte. It was an industrial town, its location on the Detroit River serving commerce rather than agriculture or recreation. Railroad tracks traversed it, carrying freight and manufactured goods far and near. Behind the Victorian "painted lady" house of multiple hues rented by the Frostics on Oak Street sat an ice cream manufacturer. Similar small businesses filled the Detroit area. Wyandotte was blue-collar, a mirror opposite of the Grosse

Pointes on the other side of downtown Detroit. The Frostic family lived here for over three decades, surrounded by other residential avenues bearing arbor-related names such as Elm, Poplar, Mulberry, and Sycamore. It was a blue-collar place, but Wyandotte held its own beauty.

Despite what some called a handicap, Gwen graduated from Theodore Roosevelt High School, the magnificent learning center her father had championed, with accolades for artistic ability.[1] She attended art school in Ypsilanti, earned a teacher's certificate, and continued her art education studies at Western State Normal School (now Western Michigan University). Feeling fulfilled, she left in 1927 without a degree. It was time to move beyond learning into doing.

To avoid burdening her parents, she set up a metalworking shop in the basement of their home, giving her enterprise the trade name "Metalcraft." In that shop—overcoming whatever disability she had—Gwen fashioned copper vases and ware that attracted the interest of Clara Ford and other society women. After her mother died in 1935, Gwen added a stationery business to metal products. She displayed a uniquely designed plastic tray at the 1939 World's Fair, then worked as a tool and die draftsperson at the famed Willow Run bomber plant during World War II. The war forced her to give up working with metal due to its designation for military purposes, but Gwen found a substitute in linoleum, not in short supply. She began to use it in the production of stationery products. Renaming the business "Presscraft Papers," she opened a shop at 200 Cedar Street in Wyandotte, with living quarters in the back.

By 1951, the printing business was a solid success and was growing a bit with each month's receipts. Gwen decided to publish a catalog to invite purchases from a wider audience. By the time of issuance of the first edition of the catalog, Fred had retired and, a widower now, decided on another move. Michigan's northwestern Lower Peninsula had always enticed him. During a visit that year near Frankfort, he decided to purchase a lot and build a cottage. Never married and without any children, Gwen was free to travel with her father as he planned his retirement home.

The north woods, so different from the farm fields of the Thumb and the Detroit area neighborhoods, enthralled her. Its rolling hills, mirror lakes, abundant orchards, quiet streams, and diverse wildlife exerted a magnetic force. Back in Wyandotte, the family had enjoyed trips to Grosse Ile, a sparsely settled island in the Detroit River. Now, Gwen discovered a place where nature was in limitless supply. She decided to close the Wyandotte shop during the summer and open one up north to serve the tourist trade. Her first northern Michigan store opened on Main Street in Frankfort during the early 1950s.

When her father died in 1954, the nearly fifty-year-old Gwen left the big city behind for good and cast her fate up north. Closing the Wyandotte shop, Gwen moved into a new, slightly larger location in Frankfort. The products she sold were not typical stationery; Gwen used her own nature designs as the foundation for the enterprise. Along with imagery of trees and streams and birds and animals, Gwen soon began to insert a few lines of her own as accompaniment to the illustrations. Just a few years after the move, associates on the state board of the National Federation of Business and Professional Women's Clubs asked Gwen to help them on a fundraiser. The result was the little hardcover book *My Michigan*.

In "a series of thoughts that may make you feel Michigan in your heart," Gwen revealed her love of the north woods. She also wove in the farm country of her youth. And she hailed urban Southeast Michigan where she had lived and worked for much of her life. She described "spans of steel" across great waterways, monuments to human conception and achievement. She praised industry, whether "intensively creative" or "very routine," for all of it had contributed to producing a high standard of living in her state. Commercial centers, whether "huge supermarkets" or "tiny creative shops," merited celebration, for they helped produce "happy luxurious living." Her work was one of celebration, of how the "doors of opportunity are open" for anyone seeking knowledge in Michigan. Reverently, she praised Michigan for offering places of communion with God.

In *My Michigan* she wrote of wildflowers growing by the roadsides all across the state, of mullein standing "like modern candelabra in the fields of snow," of "deep blue gentians." A strenuous, successful climb to a hilltop near Frankfort—perhaps at the Sleeping Bear—merited celebration: "in the company of a friend who understands," looking "over a clear blue lake—and another hill—and a larger lake beyond with golden dunes along its shore—the water and sky will merge far in the distance—as a moment of exquisite creativeness stirs the soul." Her fondness for other, less tourist-friendly locations, was also on exhibition, be it for low marshlands or "the brooks and rivers that ripple over rocky beds." A concluding stanza expressed Gwen's devotion to a place where instead of being consigned to the scrapheap, she had found an opportunity to reach her full creative potential despite physical limitations:

> One could live a lifetime in Michigan
> and still have wonder to explore . . .
> . . . for always . . . there is beauty
> for the heart that understands

The little book was a tour de force, and it led her into more writing about the place she loved so much. Bucolic Michigan provided Gwen with ever fresh and powerful inspiration. "Over the swamp," she wrote, "comes a long low call / the wind in the trees . . . Part of my soul answers to that call . . . and I am at one with loveliness." She would summarize, in words that resemble an autobiography, how "life . . . with all its beauty . . . its achievement over adversity . . . its promise of eternity . . . is taking place."

On her fifty-eighth birthday, Gwen opened another shop, this one east of Frankfort on the road to Benzonia. This place represented the full expression of Gwen's creativity. A unique design, the structure was both shop and studio, where her stationery would be produced in a setting that exhibited the amazing beauty of nature in the north woods. Its location on the Betsie River Road featured the stream meandering in its backyard, and a rustic construction that sought to blend into the landscape. During usually solitary walks in the woods nearby, she found the abundance of wildlife a special inspiration.

Out of this custom-built location she began to create more and more custom products: note cards, envelopes, postcards, calendars—all with an unmistakable style. Presscraft Papers began to publish books with Gwen's special block-print artwork and decorative frayed page ends. Sometimes the writing was simplicity itself:

> caterpillar . . . cocoon . . . butterfly—can one not believe in miracles . . . ?

At other times, it was pure elegance:

To those who see
         bare branches—
    and know they hold the buds of spring
to those who see
   stars falling in the heavens—
      and know the constellations will remain forever
         to those who see
            long lines of geese
                 fade far beyond—
      and know they come back again to nest
      to those who see
              with wonder in their hearts—
   and know—what glories there can be
            for those who see . . .

The volume *Contemplate* emerged in 1973. Its tone was surprisingly harsh. Gwen railed against the squandering of opportunity to green the environment. The voices of those trying to save marshes and wetlands, she charged, were not strong enough to counter the demands of those who wanted to fill up and develop irreplaceable sites. Cries of unemployment drowned out the pleas of those who advocated for pollution-free industry. She criticized those who were "content the earth would last their time . . . totally indifferent to what would follow after." Even with such foreboding, though, Gwen could not end on a sour note: this need not be the end, she concluded, "but a dedication to new directions."

Gwen's writing was equally prose and poetry. Her books owe much to the nature images adorning their pages, but also to the sentences and word images she crafted. Neither might have the same impact alone.

And so Gwen Frostic became well-known. Tourists beat a path to her remote door. Another catalog, bursting with paper products, brought in business from far away. The north woods, the streams, the thickets, the lakes continued to inspire her to draw and to write. By 1999 Gwen had become the creator, author, and illustrator of nearly two dozen books, with titles like *A Walk with Me* and *Wisps of Mist*. The title page of each work featured her distinctive signature, etched in bold, angular strokes. That signature also formed the main part of the sign inviting guests to visit the unique shop along the road that parallels the Betsie River.

Gwen Frostic, who had nearly died as a young girl, came to the end of her long and fruitful life on April 25, 2001. She was buried in the same Benzonia cemetery as fellow Michigan author Bruce Catton. A living witness to the triumph of the human spirit, she had been the recipient of numerous awards, honorary degrees, and other accolades. That recognition included a day named to commemorate her contributions to Michigan, and enshrinement in the Michigan Women's Hall of Fame. A fellow author called her a Michigan institution. In the early twentieth century, an institution is where she might have ended up. Instead, a loving family and her formidable will and strength of character never permitted it.

In death, Gwen Frostic had one last, unconventional contribution to make to Michigan. She gifted a large portion of her estate to the institution that hadn't even graduated her. Western Michigan University, stunned by news of the multimillion-dollar gift, responded by honoring the artist-author through its creative writing program. It holds an annual Gwen Frostic Reading Series, helping carry on her legacy of creativity. It is a legacy that is also carried on in word and image through Presscraft Papers publications that remain in print, inked on the linoleum presses that Gwen labored over for so many decades. Her life and work serve as continuing reminders to Michiganders that adversity, no matter in what shape it comes, need not be a stumbling block.

Works

My Michigan (Benzonia, MI: Presscraft Papers, 1957).

A Walk with Me (Benzonia, MI: Presscraft Papers, 1958).

These Things Are Ours (Benzonia, MI: Presscraft Papers, 1960).

To Those Who See (Benzonia, MI: Presscraft Papers, 1965).

A Place on Earth (Benzonia, MI: Presscraft Papers, ca. 1965).

Wing-borne (Benzonia, MI: Presscraft Papers, 1967).

Wisps of Mist (Benzonia, MI: Presscraft Papers, 1969).

Beyond Time (Benzonia, MI: Presscraft Papers, ca. 1971).

Contemplate (Benzonia, MI: Presscraft Papers, 1973).

The Enduring Cosmos (Benzonia, MI: Presscraft Papers, 1976).

Interlochen: An Unfinished Symphony (Benzonia, MI: Presscraft Papers, 1977).

The Infinite Destiny (Benzonia, MI: Presscraft Papers, 1978).

The Evolving Omnity (Benzonia, MI: Presscraft Papers, 1981).

The Caprice Immensity (Benzonia, MI: Presscraft Papers, 1983).

Multiversality (Benzonia, MI: Presscraft Papers, 1985).

Heuristic (Benzonia, MI: Presscraft Papers, 1987).

Chaotic Harmony (Benzonia, MI: Presscraft Papers, 1989).

Abysmal – Acumen (Benzonia, MI: Presscraft Papers, 1991).

Aggrandize (Benzonia, MI: Presscraft Papers, 1993).

Synthesis (Benzonia, MI: Presscraft Papers, 1995).

Ruminate (Benzonia, MI: Presscraft Papers, 1997).

Lilies of the Field (Benzonia, MI: Presscraft Papers, 1999).

Sites

Benzonia Township Cemetery, 8063 Love Road, Benzonia, Michigan

Gwen Frostic Prints, 5140 River Road, Beulah, Michigan 49617

Home at 355 Oak Street, in Wyandotte, Michigan

Store at 200 Cedar Street in Wyandotte, Michigan

Sculpture in Frostic Field behind Copeland Center, 2306 4th Street, Wyandotte, Michigan

Wyandotte Museum, 10 Biddle Avenue, Wyandotte, Michigan 48192 (and Bacon Library across the street)

Eugene Ruggles

Songs for the Underdog

December 4, 1935–June 3, 2004
Born in Pontiac; grew up in Macomb County and near Elk Rapids; wrote considerable poetry
about his youth on a Michigan farm and the struggles of auto industry workers.

The country around Elk Rapids, Michigan, lends itself to tourism and to agriculture. Inland there are forests and small lakes. Closer to the coast, rises formed by glaciers supply panoramic views of Lake Michigan, which tempers the nearshore climate, extending growing seasons and fostering cherry orchards.

Today the area is experiencing considerable second-home construction and hotel and restaurant growth—even in statewide economic downturns. But in the 1940s, small towns and small farms characterized the region. This was the environment of the young Eugene Ruggles, a sensitive rebel who became one of America's memorable poets. Although he has not yet had the wide recognition he deserves, he was nominated for the Pulitzer Prize for his book *The Lifeguard in the Snow*. Critic Joseph Garrison of Mary Baldwin College said of the volume, "In rich images and lines from the wood of the heart, Ruggles warms us."

Eugene Ruggles (far left) in childhood with his family in Macomb County, where the family lived before moving near Elk Rapids. In the later farm setting, natural beauty and vivid scenes of farm life contrasted with his father's harshness, both of which contributed to his poetry. Photo courtesy of Delia Moon.

Born in Pontiac in 1935, Ruggles moved with his family in 1945 from Macomb County to a farm six miles north of Elk Rapids. Like his four siblings, he attended the small Elk Rapids school, built in 1874. His brother Glenn said the children thought they had found paradise in the liberty and beauty of their farm surroundings. There was room and space to breathe, and opportunities for small-town pranks—some of which were not well received. Ruggles and friends once hot-wired the principal's auto to travel twenty miles to a football game.

Underneath apparently simple and romanticized rural life there is often pain and complexity. In a late-life poem, Ruggles called himself "the last of five children from parents who never sang / they broke their lives over each other until they ended." His father frequently raged and periodically beat him, helping shape the future poet's empathy for the underdog. Later in life he would tell his brother that their father was the most powerful influence on his life. Ruggles could never complete a poem about this man, getting only as far as one line: "My father I am digging toward you."

But Eugene's youth inspired generous amounts of verse on other subjects. Much of his poetry captured the vivid experience and imagery of the farm. As in "The Harness":

My mother churning butter
between her knees
on the porch of the farmhouse
there is no sound of the steps,
only a small boy dragging a harness
heaped across the short grass.

And in "The Horses":

The sun is wet over their backs
it flows along the veins of the harness
and falls from their necks and thighs
into the dry earth where the hoof prints
sinking behind them
have been dusted like bricks by the robes of hay.

One poem written decades later fondly recalled a hired man from the farm. "Eben Dawson's Gift" cites the kindly man's habit of driving to the city every Christmas Day to find an unfortunate driver's vehicle to push from the snow, or to help reignite a battery. Invited to go along, Ruggles would run to the truck. The poem acknowledged that Eben had once saved the young Ruggles's life and had taught the boy "to be with horses." Remembering Eben's laugh, Ruggles ends the poem near a cemetery in drifting snow, thinking back on the man forty years later and saying, "I would still run . . . to his truck."

In 1979, Ruggles told an interviewer that the farm and small-town life of northern Michigan deeply influenced his poetry. "Everything was physical, the farm life, milking ten cows every morning. I didn't feel lonely at all. I used to love the long bus ride to school and the sporting events in other small towns."

After completing his high school studies, Ruggles hitchhiked across the United States, playing pool and piecing together a living from an assortment of jobs. "It was an adventure. I was hungry for everything, very hungry." He attended Wayne State University and Northern Michigan University— although even his family wasn't sure he ever obtained his bachelor's degree. He received considerable value at Northern, even if not the degree. A professor, Earl Hilton, encouraged his writing and developed a rapport with

Ruggles that the poet long remembered and cherished. Poems inspired by his time in Marquette describe, among other things, the cold majesty of Lake Superior and of northern Michigan's defining season, winter.

In the 1960s, Ruggles moved his wife and three young children from Michigan to California. In San Francisco his literary influence grew and his political activism quickened. Eugene's poetry now spanned half a continent. His art and personal commitment embraced protest against the abandonment of the poor, discrimination against racial minorities, war, and workers dispossessed by the rapid disintegration of the auto industry in Michigan.

He organized poetry-reading fundraisers for Amnesty International, opponents of the Vietnam War, and the Native American takeover of Alcatraz Island. Brother Glenn said that one benefit for the Native Americans of Alcatraz raised "$800 and one milk goat." The readings were not dry, academic events. Featuring Gary Snyder, Robert Bly, and other celebrated American poets, they abounded with energy, advocacy, and humor.

Before a 1979 reading in Traverse City, Ruggles observed that over time "Poets have been foremost among the voices that attempt to preserve and protect human dignity. Human freedom. And future generations. The children." And so his poetry celebrated those who stood their ground on principle and in defense of their humanity. He cheered for Rosa Parks, the famous civil rights icon who refused to go to the back of the bus in Montgomery, Alabama. The 1985 poem is "You May Do That," the words Parks spoke to the bus driver who threatened to have her arrested. In another poem, he indicted America for its treatment of minority peoples, from African Americans to Native Americans. In the wake of the filmed police beating of African American Rodney King, which triggered a deadly Los Angeles riot in 1992, he wrote "You and Rodney King."

> As you did with the Native Americans,
> you have now put the African Americans
> on reservations, this time in the inner city,
>> to die. This time there are more of them.

Another poem cherished the work and memory of Dorothy Day, famed cofounder of the Catholic Worker movement, which undertook direct aid to, and social activism on behalf of, the homeless and poor. "There is nothing between you / And any of the lords today," he wrote of her funeral.

Eugene Ruggles and daughter Anna in approximately 1990. Fashioning poetry out of hard times for Detroit auto workers and the heroism of civil rights pioneers, Ruggles was lauded by Lawrence Ferlinghetti, who called the Michigan man's work "an important contribution to our poetry culture." Courtesy of Delia Moon.

One poem, "Masses," was rumored to have ornamented the wall of Vice President Walter Mondale's office in the 1970s. "Who will speak for the simple and dumb . . ." Joy and celebration also characterized some of his other poetry. He told stories of romantic and family love, natural beauty, wry humor about human nature, and grace in aging.

In 1970 he moved to the California country, to the famous Wheeler Ranch commune and thence to Delia Moon's ranch in Bodega, where he built a cabin of wood. Known for his unruly, curly hair, flannel shirts, and work boots, he associated with the beat poets, such as Allen Ginsburg and Lawrence Ferlinghetti. But more discerning readers recognized that his deep imagery made him akin to poets such as Robert Bly, James Wright, and William Stafford. Gene's work and reputation helped him receive writing grants from the National Institute of Arts and Letters, the National Endowment for the Arts, the American Academy of Arts and Letters, the Academy of American Poets, and the Sonoma Community Foundation.

Ruggles's mercurial temperament, alcohol abuse, and perhaps the memory of the tortured relationship with his own father caused family difficulties. Two of his offspring did not attend his memorial. Members of his extended family back in Michigan, however, recalled late-in-life, late-night phone calls (ignoring the three-hour time difference) in which he expounded on his thoughts, feelings, and creative work.

Because his only steady paying job had been a five-year stint with the merchant marine, money was never plentiful. In his final years, living solely on disability payments, Ruggles struggled to stay afloat financially. He also struggled physically, using a walker because of defective hips, and undergoing open-heart and hip surgery. Years of heavy drinking had also undermined his health.

Shortly before his death in 2004, Ruggles was evicted from his fifteen-year living space in the Petaluma Hotel. His many friends came through, helping him find a new apartment. "I love this place," he said of his neighborhood. "All I need is a river and a good bookstore, and I feel good," he told a reporter, who described Ruggles as "a major force on the Bay Area's literary scene" for decades.

Upon his death, literary executor Delia Moon published *Roads of Bread*, a collection of more than two hundred of his poems. They included the previously published "The Lifeguard in the Snow," a manila envelope with poems he still considered unfinished, and the volume he was crafting at his death, called *Enough*.

Ruggles returned again and again to scenes of urban Detroit and Flint, where workers paid the penalty for a floundering economy and the poor judgment of management. Ruggles had toiled in Detroit factories in his youth and identified viscerally with the suffering of former assembly-line workers turned out of their jobs. Over a quarter of a century after its creation, "The Unemployed Automobile Workers of Detroit Prepare to Spend Christmas Standing in Line," Ruggles's poem of industrial heartbreak, still resonated in a faltering state economy.

> It's December, nearly Christmas. Nineteen eighty-three.
> The Detroit River is choked with ice. Woodward Avenue
> is empty of cars and flowing with a foot of snow . . .
> The bar is long and empty, the bartender hands me a glass
> saying he's been waiting months for GM to call him back.
> A black man comes in to cash his unemployment check.

"His work will pass on into the American canon," said one friend at his death. Lawrence Ferlinghetti, in a personal note to his publisher, called Ruggles's works "an important contribution to our poetry culture."

Ruggles's poems sometimes spoke of matters distant from Michigan, but remained rooted in an outlook shaped by his childhood in the Wolverine State. Unflinching in their portrayal of family tragedy, passionate political action, and social decay, Ruggles's poems have their source in a fundamentally American character, shaped by the alternately gentle and brutal hands of Michigan.

Works

The Lifeguard in the Snow (Pittsburgh: University of Pittsburgh Press, 1977).
"From Spending the Sun" (unpublished poem).
"Enough" (unpublished poem).
(All collected, along with unfinished poems, in *Roads of Bread: The Collected Poems of Eugene Ruggles*, edited by Delia Moon [Bodega, CA: Petaluma River Press, 2009]).

Sites

Farm country north of the Village of Elk Rapids
Shuttered General Motors Pontiac Assembly Plant, 2100 South Opdyke Road, Pontiac.

Upper Peninsula

Carroll Watson Rankin

Northern Light

May 11, 1864–August 13, 1945

Born and lived in Marquette nearly her entire life

· ·

Little things count for a great deal in this world, sometimes . . . —*DANDELION COTTAGE*

Sometimes they do. Especially when societal conventions limit a writer's world.

Caroline Clement Watson—affectionately known as "Carrie"—was born in Marquette, Michigan, the youngest of ten children, during the penultimate year of the American Civil War. Nestled on the southern Lake Superior shore, Marquette was a small town in 1864. In Watson's youth, it had only one of each kind of store and, as she later recounted, two drugstores of which only one sold soda water and neither sold ice cream sodas. Ladies did not walk on the side of Front Street where the saloons were. By the end of the century, iron ore mining and transshipment made Marquette an economic powerhouse, a city of culture, and a travel destination. Carrie's parents, Jonas and Emily Watson, had relocated to the Upper Peninsula from Ireland and had taken over management of the struggling general store. Life became profitable for the Watson clan; they could afford

Caroline Clement Watson as a young woman. She employed a *nom de plume* to get published while a full-time wife and mother at the turn of the twentieth century in the Upper Peninsula. Courtesy of the J.M. Longyear Research Library.

a house overlooking the lake, and a sailboat to skipper for picnics on the nearby shores.

Marquette owes its existence to the discovery of rich ores in the surrounding countryside, and its frontage on a lee shore of an unpredictable freshwater ocean. Included in the exchange of Toledo for the Upper Peninsula during Michigan's campaign for statehood, the town began to thrive as soon as iron shipments commenced in the middle 1800s. With associated wealth came the trappings of culture found in much larger population centers. Today, a silent ore dock looming in the middle of town symbolizes its past, just as grander architecture in the form of a courthouse, public library, hotel, city hall, and cathedral represent a promising future built on solid foundations. The town retains a quaintness derived from a much simpler era.

By age four, Carrie Watson had begun to use lead pencils and 10-yard strips of white paper from ribbon bolts to write picture stories. Unfortunately, the socially imposed career prospects for a young woman in the nineteenth-century Upper Peninsula were essentially two: marriage or spinsterhood.

Four more decades would pass before women gained the vote. Two decades more would pass before Rosie the Riveter revolutionized gender roles. Carrie had to invent an opportunity to achieve her vision for life.

At eleven, she published a short story in a periodical for young people called *What Next*. Although Carrie believed the journal published nearly anything that came in "over the transom," this small success spurred her on. By fifteen, she had stories published in several religious papers and magazines. Attending school in Scotland, Wisconsin, and Chicago stiffened her resolve. She was sixteen when the *Marquette Daily Mining Journal* advertised for "a bright boy to do reporting." Carrie applied—acknowledging the gender issue, but claiming eligibility as "bright"—and, against the odds, secured a post at the paper. For the next six years, she wrote articles for the *Journal* and rose to become society editor, until marriage in 1886 meant retirement from journalism.

Wedding bells did not, however, sound the end of Carrie's writing. The marriage to Ernest Rankin produced three daughters and a son. After a decade, married life and prior experience inspired her to write pieces for garden magazines and women's publications like *Ladies Home Journal*. She became a prolific writer published by a wide range of periodicals, her work initially appearing under the byline "C.W. Rankin." One evening at dinner, to settle down the children, she fashioned a story; their enthusiastic reaction led her to reduce it to paper and submit it to *Youth's Companion*. When a $40 check arrived in the mail, together with an invitation to write more young people's stories, Carrie—now under the pen name "Carroll"—discovered a new outlet for her creativity on behalf of younger generations. She sent off stories to leading magazines of the era—*Century, Harper's Monthly, St. Nicholas, Leslie's, Lippincott's, Metropolitan*—and enjoyed seeing her children and their friends find them in print. One month, eleven Rankin stories were published. Her children reported that their mother wrote all the time.

One day, a daughter protested that all the reading material in all the world suitable for her age and gender had been exhausted; why didn't Mother do something about it? Carrie answered the challenge. Sitting with a pencil and pad of paper that evening on the porch of their home on Ridge Street, she began to dash off sheets in rapid-fire fashion for a new piece of fiction. The story had its basis in gardening: a community effort to rid front lawns of unsightly weeds. Handing each sheet to the complainant, Eleanor, she found that the story appealed both to the girl and several friends who appeared and began to share in the tale as it unfolded page by page. Over the next several evenings, until the writing pad was used up, woman and children shared together as a story captivated all of them. Seven chapters were done, and Carrie saved the work in case it might come in handy someday.

In early 1904, a letter arrived from leading publisher Henry Holt and Company requesting something longer than a magazine article, something of particular interest to young women. Mrs. Rankin had one, of course, well underway. Taking the seven chapters and adding another dozen, she completed the book in April and sent it off. A month expired. While she was making muffins in her kitchen one afternoon, a telegram arrived—usually a sign of bad news—surprising her with notification of the book's acceptance. She really couldn't stop to celebrate, "but the muffins were all right."

The book, *Dandelion Cottage*, was all right, too, and found a new audience well beyond the front porch in Marquette. Set near the turn of the century in "Lakeville, a thriving Northern Michigan town," the book told the story of four girls, ages twelve to fourteen, who were allowed the run of a derelict church-owned structure for a summer playhouse. To earn rent to pay for the cottage, the girls had to bring its grounds into reputable shape. The structure took its name from the "great, fluffy, golden dandelions" that filled the cottage yard—and the source of work by which the girls were able to gain possession. The book featured their enjoyment in making it habitable, of making real the fantasy of having their very own house all to themselves, and it took them through a storyline of challenge, disappointment, displacement, and ultimate reconciliation.

The *Marquette Journal* regarded it as "a juvenile book written mainly to attract girls, but motives of kindly interest will greatly broaden the circle of its readers in Marquette county." It would do well, as "her success in juvenile literature has been pronounced." The *New York Times* on December 10, 1904, judged it "a very pleasant story," "well told," "thoroughly healthful, quite free from the mawkish sentiment too often disfiguring stories for the young." The *Times* reviewer went on to damn it with faint praise: "There is nothing to be said against such books except that they serve to shut out real literature from young minds, and, in the end, to dull the taste for the books that live."

The Dandelion Cottage in Marquette made immortal by a mother's imagination and storytelling skill.
Photo by Jack Dempsey.

An interesting phrase, "books that live." The December 30, 1911, edition of *The Publishers' Weekly* announced amazing news about issuance of a 10th edition of *Dandelion Cottage*. It said Carroll Watson Rankin might be considered to have "arrived" as a favorite author for girls. Her fame extended beyond the Superior coast to one farther west, for the 1922 annual meeting report of the California Library Association referred to "the well known books of Carroll Rankin."

In 1946, forty years after its first appearance, Holt republished the novel, replacing the five original illustrations with pen and ink drawings more appropriate for a mid-twentieth-century edition. The American Institute of Graphic Arts favored its new design and "particularly decorative cover and end papers." It was the story within, however, that continued to draw readership. After passage of another thirty years, the Marquette Historical Society obtained rights to the revised book and has, since 1977, published six editions. The original went through three times as many; a new edition of the book in 1946 garnered more. The book, still in print, features the original dedication to three daughters, a listing of "The Persons of the Story," and "Contents." And it remains a favorite for those who find its simple charm compelling, a heartwarming read that hearkens back to childhood, to before the unsettledness of a postmodern twenty-first century. A juvenile book? Perhaps, more accurately, a book that appeals to the young heart in a reader of any age.

A century after the first edition appeared in Marquette, at the opposite end of the state in a middle-class suburban Detroit house, a frayed copy of *Dandelion Cottage*, containing many loose, well-worn pages, lays on a shelf. The book had been the property of a young woman, herself a mother and then grandmother to a little girl named Diane. The latter remembered paying childhood visits in the care of her mother, Marjorie, to the old woman, who enjoyed letting her read the book and share in the common pleasure of this flight of imagination. On that shelf, inside the front cover, remains this precious inscription: "From Mama to M"—from the original owner to Marjorie. Preserved fondly and bearing testimony to many trips through its pages, the book exemplifies the devotion of several generations of female Michiganders to this "very pleasant story." It is the Diane's "favorite book in the world"—her "most treasured possession." It is, truly, a book that lives.

One might assume that *Dandelion Cottage* originated from purely an imaginary place, but not so: the cottage was real and remains in existence. Built around 1880 as a sexton's house, the structure was originally located next to Marquette's St. Paul Episcopal Church on High Street. In 1888 a leading citizen, Peter White, donated it to the church on condition that the house be relocated. Moved just a few feet to nearby Arch Street, the modest home stood for nearly a century until the church decided to virtually give it away, requiring only that it be relocated once again. The place was in sad shape, and no takers appeared. Finally, Marquette's mayor purchased it for $1 and moved it down the street to 440 East Arch. There it still stands, retaining much of its historic nature after interior renovations and exterior conservation, marked by bright yellow siding and green trim to match its name. In 1992 it went on the state historical register. In 1993 the author's surviving daughter affixed a historical marker near the front door. Arch Street is not far from downtown Marquette; the cottage seems not far from when the story was written, despite the passage of time.

About the same time that *Dandelion Cottage* was published, at the other end of the St. Lawrence River watershed, on Prince Edward Island, another female author was working on a book about an eleven-year-old girl. She would entitle it *Anne of Green Gables*. Similar stories centering on young people as heroes, heroines, protagonists, would appear in succeeding decades and be purchased in droves—such as inventor Tom Swift, cultural icons the Hardy Boys, and detectives Nancy Drew and Trixie Belden. The Newbery Medal winner for 1904 was a fanciful book called *The Marvelous Land of Oz*. Each had its devoted following. Each has achieved a form of immortality.

What of the little thing entitled *Dandelion Cottage*? The creative center-piece of the story was, in Rankin's own words, a small thing: "It started as a true story, but no story teller can be trusted to stick to the exact truth—his pencil runs away with him. There was a cottage, there were four little girls, and there were dandelions, but all the rest was cut from whole cloth." The little dwelling, dilapidated and careworn, somehow served as inspiration for a flight of fancy. Rankin's life as a mother in Marquette, striving to meet the intellectual and emotional needs of her little girls at the turn of one century into another, yielded the substance of the story. It was not autobiography; it was a novel grounded in a certain timelessness.

Simplicity would be back in vogue a century later, after the breakneck pace of American life taxed many people beyond their natural capacities. Cottage living made a comeback, with its connotations of harmony and community. When Rankin began to write with pencil on pad on the front porch of her Upper Peninsula home, humanity had yet to march off to the War to End All Wars, yet to experience an economic collapse that shook the pillars of the Western World, yet to encounter a global conflagration marked by the Holocaust. A twenty-one-chapter book about four girls in a tiny rundown cottage and their joy, heartbreak, and triumph may seem trite and naive in these advanced times. Perhaps a song from the Flower Power era puts it in perspective:

What are we in time going by
The simple story of a younger life
Happy dreams and somehow through the day
We haven't come so far to lose our way
—Mountain, "For Yasgur's Farm"

Rankin wrote a sequel, *The Adopting of Rosa Marie*, along with several more in the Dandelion Cottage series. She authored ten books to go with columns and articles written from a very young age on, until her death a week after the end of World War II. She was buried in Park Cemetery in Marquette, in the community where she had lived nearly her entire life. Her works might have been regarded by some as all little things, really. Settings in the books were familiar to Upper Peninsula readers, reminiscent of the Native American encampment up the Little Garlic River in *The Castaways of Peter's Patch*, and the huckleberry picnics near the Sand River in *Finders Keepers*. All were sited in the Marquette area.

Just one of her works has lasted in print up to the present. Such a legacy might not be enough to categorize it as "immortal." For those who open up to its enchantment, Rankin's first novel continues to count for a great deal in a world where the lasting importance of adolescent innocence ought not be devalued.

Works

Dandelion Cottage (New York: Henry Holt and Co., 1904).

The Girls of Gardenville (New York: Henry Holt and Co., 1906).

The Anti Foster Pet Association (New York: Henry Holt and Co., 1907).

The Adopting of Rosa Marie (New York: Henry Holt and Co., 1908).

Castaways of Pete's Patch (New York: Henry Holt and Co., 1911).

The Cinder Pond (New York: Henry Holt and Co., 1915).

Girls of Highland Hall (New York: Henry Holt and Co., 1921).

Gipsy Nan (New York: Henry Holt and Co., 1926).

Finders Keepers (New York: Henry Holt and Co., 1930).

Wolf Rock (New York: Henry Holt and Co., 1933).

Stump Village (New York: Henry Holt and Co., 1935).

Sites

Dandelion Cottage, 440 East Arch Street, Marquette, Michigan 49855

Home at 219 East Ridge Street, Marquette, Michigan

Landmark Hotel ("Dandelion Cottage" room), 230 North Front Street, Marquette, Michigan 49855

Marquette County Historical Museum, 213 North Front Street, Marquette, Michigan 49855

Park Cemetery, north of Ridge and west of Seventh; Michigan, Ohio, and Hewitt Streets end at the cemetery; entrance on North Seventh Street, Marquette, Michigan

John Donaldson Voelker

Great Character

June 29, 1903–March 18, 1991
Born in Ishpeming; graduate of Ishpeming High School; degrees from Northern State Normal School
and the University of Michigan; nearly lifelong resident of Marquette County

. . . .

"I didn't like cities. I hate to even see them," growled John Donaldson
Voelker in a 1990 interview. "I think they are uninhabitable."

Urban areas are scarce in Michigan's Upper Peninsula. Mostly rural,
its largest city is Marquette, with some 20,000 inhabitants. Voelker was
a native of Ishpeming, located several miles to the west, an even smaller
municipality. Disdain for big city life might be expected from one who
grew up in a land teeming with trees and lakes, not with people. Ishpeming
is no Four Corners, however, and it was city people who made Voelker an
author of national fame. The Upper Peninsula is a more complex place,
with more complicated influence, than common wisdom might have it.

The product of an unlikely marriage between a music teacher and a tall
German saloonkeeper, this youngest of six sons was born in 1903 in an old
frame house a block from the Carnegie Library in Ishpeming. Its proximity
proved fortunate. The building and its stacks of books elevated the lives of
Ishpeming's mineworker families during the late nineteenth and early

twentieth centuries, and Voelker's mother encouraged his traipsing over to the classically designed structure at Main and Barnum Streets. Many days found the boy roaming the shelves in order to, as he later summarized, "read, read, read." Poring through Mark Twain, Horatio Alger, and other forms of popular fiction enticed him into a lifelong love of words. His father's saloon, a favored resource in the mining community, was the other place where he found joy. Here he listened to life accounts not so sanitized as Alger, not so innocent as Parson Weems's biography of Washington, but equally compelling.

Reading and storytelling propelled him to nearby Northern State Normal School in Marquette (now Northern Michigan University) and then the University of Michigan Law School downstate in Ann Arbor. During this venture into the populated Lower Peninsula, he met the woman he would marry, a native of Ernest Hemingway's Illinois hometown of Oak Park. After a couple of difficult years apart, Grace prevailed upon her father to secure a job for her young lawyer friend at Mayer, Meyer, Austrian & Platt, one of Chicago's premier law firms (still in existence). Voelker spent three years in the "bullpen" researching the law and supporting the experienced attorneys who tried cases. He never saw the inside of a courtroom. The stories being written were those of other lawyers; the realization came to him that fashioning his own would make him much happier.

Escaping the Windy City with his young bride for what became a permanent return to the north country, Voelker opened a law office in the old Woolworth building in Ishpeming. The Depression was in full force, and private practice was a hardscrabble life in the Upper Peninsula. He soon decided that the prospect of a steady income made running for public office attractive, believing that a hometown boy could use his origins as a successful platform. To the surprise of many—including himself—Voelker won the 1934 election for county prosecutor. At the tender age of thirty-one, with little actual courtroom experience, he embarked on a fourteen-year-long stint as prosecuting attorney for Marquette County, the largest county east of the Mississippi. He would try every kind of case, encounter every type of crime, confront every type of criminal during the next decade and a half. Every couple of years, he would need to campaign in the small towns, ubiquitous bars, mine entrances, and other public venues where the U.P. voter could be found. Finally defeated for reelection by a slim margin in 1948, Voelker discovered he had tired of the job. Deciding against a recount, he turned to other interests.

Free from the dictates of public office, he first went hunting for uranium among the rocks and vales of the Upper Peninsula, because the mineral was valuable to America's post–World War II national defense. His Geiger counter, purchased on the installment plan, as were so many products during those boom years, turned up thorium—a powerful radioactive material that outstripped contemporary scientific knowledge of how to convert it to safe use. After this failure, he was asked to go back into public service and run for Congress. Being a good Democratic soldier, he assented—but this effort, too, was unsuccessful. Voelker went back to private practice, somewhat fatalistic about what the unpromising future might hold.

One saving grace in these failures was the time they preserved for fishing. Writing and practicing law were worthwhile, but for Voelker nothing could compare to the honorable and ancient sport of angling. To be a true Yooper, one either fished or hunted. Voelker found much joy from hook and line. The law put food on the table for his substantial family, but it hardly consumed his interest.

Then, a spark from the Northern Lights fell to earth. A war veteran who had been accused of murdering his wife's assailant in nearby Big Bay retained Voelker as defense counsel. The trial was full of scandal, and this was the 1950s—an era of separate beds for television couples, and reference to "in the family way" for pregnancy. Involving an assault on a married woman, "unmentionables," and physical evidence that rarely saw the light of day, the trial—which Voelker won—had the makings of great drama. It might make a great book if one were a writer and had a publisher. Which, due to a few paltry-selling volumes, Voelker already was and had.

While serving as prosecutor and with a growing family to support, Voelker put pen to paper and began to write, instead of legal briefs and memorandums, stories having their roots in the law and the Upper Peninsula. His serious attempts at writing had begun when he was twelve years old, followed by magazine articles during the first two years after law school before moving to Chicago. He published three books, two about criminal practice. One, *Danny and the Boys*, told tales of a Yooper fishing guide and his boisterous

Voelker fishing on the Escanaba River as a young man, employing a hand-rolled Parodi cigar to ward off the flies and mosquitoes. Courtesy of the Voelker Family, Kitchie Hill, Inc.

buddies, a cast of characters identifiable by their Upper Peninsula origins. As Voelker would say later, these books "died a natural death" and produced little notice and lesser income. The lurid trial gave him the substance of a more powerful novel, and the work he called *Anatomy of a Murder* was born with only three months' effort. It would change his life.

Because of concern that voters would believe he was giving the prosecutor's job short shrift if they discovered he was novel-writing while on the public payroll, Voelker had settled on a *nom de plume* to conceal his identity. Taking his mother's maiden name—Traver, pronounced with a long "a"—and the first name of a deceased brother, Voelker found a New York publisher for *Anatomy* in 1957. Robert Traver would soon be a name on the *Times* bestseller list.

About the same time as the book was in the final stages of publication, an opening occurred on Michigan's highest—indeed, only—appellate court.

Having made acquaintance with one of Michigan's U.S. senators and other key party leaders, such as Governor G. Mennen Williams, Voelker received an appointment and took his seat on the high court in Lansing on New Year's Day, 1957. As Justice, his opinions had distinction, not so much in erudition as in style. In one of the most famous, required by a case where police unlawfully raided a naturist camp despite the lack of outsider complaints, Voelker wrote that he was unwilling "to burn down the house of constitutional safeguards in order to roast a few nudists." One unfortunate precedent to the contrary he "nominated for oblivion." A situation with little precedent was a "rather misty area of the law." He withheld approval of an argument thusly: "To such a situation we will not give our grace." Within a year of his appointment, however, Mr. Traver's fame eclipsed Mr. Justice's.

It might be hard to believe, in today's media-inflamed world, that a backwoods prosecutor could write a tale of the courtroom that would capture national attention. That's just what happened. The Traver book became a Book-of-the-Month Club selection, climbed the bestseller lists and stayed there for sixty-six weeks, and proceeded through four hardcover and ten paperback editions. *Anatomy* might well be regarded as a precursor to the modern legal courtroom thriller, giving rise to the likes of Turow, Grisham, and Martini. The *New York Times* reviewer was captivated: "Rarely have I been so entertained . . . it held me as few books have, I couldn't put it down. The style is simple, colloquial English, beautifully adapted to its task, and often pungently effective."[1] The reading public concurred, buying up 4.6 million copies in hardcover and paperback within the first two years it appeared.

Anatomy was such a sensation that famed movie director Otto Preminger secured the movie rights and, to most observers' surprise, determined to make the film on location in the Upper Peninsula. The principal location was Marquette County, especially the courthouse with its striking dome, stonework, and hilltop setting. In a community struggling during an economic downturn, the invasion from Hollywood was welcomed with open arms for its dollars and its diversions. Academy Award–winner James Stewart played the folksy ex-prosecutor—essentially the Voelker character, only partly disguised in the book. Lee Remick played the victim, Ben Gazzara was the defendant, and George C. Scott turned in a typically strong performance—though, as in the book, Scott's character, the assistant attorney general from the state capital (Lansing), brought in to aid the inexperienced new local DA, was defeated by Stewart in the jury verdict. (Thus, in double irony, Voelker enjoyed seeing the overmatched Upper Peninsula ex-DA whip the downstate big city wunderkind on the page and the screen.) People and production made their mark on the normally cynical Yoopers.

The 1959 movie, sticking largely to the book, has been regarded as one of the most accurate and compelling courtroom dramas ever made. Filming on location may have helped, for sets like the Big Bay Tavern added authenticity that a Hollywood backlot could not. The film won seven Academy Awards, remarkable for any motion picture. The author so thoroughly enjoyed the experience that he helped out Preminger in a trailer for the film. His rough-hewn voice was quite a contrast to the German director's tenor.

Late that year, John Voelker, now fifty-six, decided the trips down to the state capital in Lansing for court proceedings (made easier by the opening of the Mackinac Bridge in the year of his appointment, a development he was not sanguine about) were not nearly as compelling as life in the Upper Peninsula now that his financial future seemed secure. To the surprise of many in the legal community, he chucked his justiceship, fled the capital, and elected to stay home. Freed from the demands of the courthouse, back home he could fish, play cribbage as the unofficial champion of the peninsula, and write as he cared to. Or all three at once. Using legal pads to sketch out his stories, editing them with inserts and deletions like legal briefs, Voelker spent the next two decades penning several more works of legal fiction along with books on his inescapable passion. *Trout Madness* and *Trout Magic*, and one stolen from his mother lode—*Anatomy of a Fisherman*—appealed to anglers caught in the mania of luring the denizens of glorious rivers and streams. They also hooked the imagination of readers whom Voelker took down two-tracks into Michigan trout streams and into the challenge and joy of fly-fishing.

The postjudicial U.P. routine fit him to a tee. Breakfast, followed by a trip to the post office for the mail, then a stop at a local watering hole for a game or two of cribbage, after which came a drive out to a certain rural pond down and off a lonely county road where, as if at the end of the rainbow, a treasure awaited. Voelker called the spot, spring-fed and completely

John Voelker engaged in two of his favorite things at Frenchman's Pond, a mystery fishing hole and writing den in the central Upper Peninsula. Courtesy of Frederick M. Baker, Jr.

remote, "Frenchman's Pond," and most good days would find him in a contest with the plentiful but not always cooperative brook trout. Way out in the woods, this natural cathedral was hemmed in by pine and hemlock, where old church pews allowed the congregants to worship in ways mystical and restorative, where inspiration would yield Voelker's own *Testament.*

When the fishing was done, he'd head home in late afternoon to Grace and the girls, until the daughters grew up and moved away. Then, it was the two of them, an old-fashioned or two, and reading or gaming into the night. Writing filled in the cracks, yielding seven more books.

Voelker always wrote about what he knew. He knew the courtroom and penned the first great American legal novel. He knew the peculiar people of this sparsely populated northern peninsula, and they found their way onto a legal pad. He knew the backwoods, and the two-track, and the pine and scrub brush. He knew the never-ending contest in fly casting, the duel with elusive creatures on many a day. Just as writing is a solitary art, so is fishing. Both braced him.

Voelker brought the territory above the Bridge to many readers in many cities. He brought them to Detroit and to Chicago in the Midwest. Thanks to *Anatomy* and the motion picture, folks in New York City and Los Angeles also learned about the Upper Peninsula. One of those Big Apple-ites was Charles Kuralt. For decades he reported for CBS television in the "On the Road with . . ." series. Vignettes about America and its characters made the segment a highly popular part of the evening news and special programming. Kuralt met Voelker during one of his cross-country trips, and the outcome was more than just a single episode. The two hit it off; Kuralt returned to fish with his friend and to enjoy the pristine backwoods of Michigan's Upper Peninsula. The craggy reporter found a soul mate in Superior country.

In many ways, John Voelker was a classic embodiment of Michigan's Upper Peninsula. He would regularly knock off from work to go fishing. He enjoyed the conviviality of the saloon, a legacy of boyhood in his father's establishment. He relished storytelling. And he loved putting stories on paper for those too far away to spend time north of the Bridge. To think of Voelker is to envision a red flannel shirt, knotty pine walls, pockets full of fishing lures, thimbleberry jam. Of a wood-sided station wagon, Kromer hat, and a tin cup full of bracing spring water. Of a well-used cast-iron frying pan, a cabin window open and a sun-faded curtain wafting on the breeze, a wood stove and a crackling fire on a cool fall evening. Of place names in the county he served and wrote about, like the Yellow Dog Plains, Sawmill River, National Mine, Big Bay, and Frenchman's Pond. All true. But not the whole truth and nothing but the truth.

To regard the Upper Peninsula as a northern Appalachia, overrun with antisocial misanthropes who prefer days' old growth of whiskers and evening-long encounters with whiskey over polite society, is to throw the line into the part of the river where it must snag. The peninsula hosts centers of learning, a university and colleges, libraries and collections. It boasts museums and local history societies. Its cultural artifacts are everywhere. Most of all, to be of the U.P. is to have an identity, a membership card in a community that, alone across Michigan's diverse geography, entitles one to feel at home just by being there. John Voelker acted the curmudgeon, and one could regard him as the prototypical Yooper. Inside lurked a mind and talent for writing that could have succeeded on either right or left ocean coast.

Today, Ishpeming and Marquette are posts on the Iron Ore Heritage Trail, a multiple-use route that winds through the Marquette Iron Range for nearly fifty miles from Lake Superior inland to Republic, linking towns, communities, historic locations, and tales of the people of yesteryear. John Voelker was one of those unique Upper Peninsula assets. A storyteller of a vanishing breed, he lived and fished and wrote in one of the world's most beautiful natural settings. He lived to be a crusty old coot, but he held the respect and affection of people across the state and nation.

"There used to be characters all over. Characters are disappearing, the local ones. They're out-talked by the TV and the rest of it. It's changed. Hard to find, they're in nursing homes or dead or something. The place was crawling with them when I was a kid. I was attracted to them."[2]

In the spring of 1991, Voelker succumbed to time. He was still active at eighty-seven, enjoying fishing and Michigan and its people. Upon his burial in the Ishpeming Cemetery, one of the great characters of the Upper Peninsula disappeared from the scene. The books he wrote—legal novels and fly-fishing stories—are still crawling with them.

Works

. . . .

Trouble-Shooter: The Story of a Northwoods Prosecutor (New York: Viking Press, 1943).

Danny and the Boys: Being Some Legends of Hungry Hollow (Cleveland: World Publishing Co., 1951; Detroit: Wayne State University, 1987).

Small Town D.A. (New York: E.P. Dutton, 1954; London: Faber and Faber, 1959).

Anatomy of a Murder (New York: St. Martin's Press, 1958, 1983; Pleasantville, NY: ImPress Mystery, 2000).

Trout Madness (New York: St. Martin's Press, 1960; Santa Barbara: Peregrine Smith, 1979; New York: Simon & Schuster, 1989).

Hornstein's Boy (New York: St. Martin's Press, 1962).

Anatomy of a Fisherman (New York: McGraw-Hill, 1964; Santa Barbara: Peregrine Smith, 1978).

Laughing Whitefish (New York: McGraw-Hill, 1965; New York: St. Martin's Press, 1983; East Lansing: Michigan State University Press, 2011).

The Jealous Mistress (Boston: Little, Brown and Co., 1967).

Trout Magic (New York: Crown Publishers, 1974; Salt Lake City: Peregrine Smith
Books, 1983; New York: Simon & Schuster, 1989).
People versus Kirk (New York: St. Martin's Press, 1981).
*Traver on Fishing: A Treasury of Robert Traver's Finest Stories and Essays about
Fishing for Trout* (Guilford, CT: Lyons Press, 2001).

Sites

Childhood home, 205 West Barnum Street, Ishpeming, Michigan
Ishpeming Carnegie Public Library, 317 North Main Street, Ishpeming,
Michigan 49849
Ishpeming Cemetery, 1705 North Second Street, Ishpeming, MI
Landmark Inn, 230 North Front Street, Marquette, MI 49855 (to stay in the
Voelker room)
LumberJack Tavern, 202 Bensinger, Big Bay, Michigan 49808
Marquette County Courthouse, 234 West Baraga Avenue, Marquette,
Michigan 49855

Notes

George Matthew Adams: "Today's Talk"

1. The "sites" listed in this volume for each author include the homes, offices, and other structures in which they lived, worked, and wrote, along with other locations that helped provide inspiration or are in some way connected to their lives or their deaths.

Kenyon, Frost, and Miller: Arbor Days

1. *Oxford Companion to Twentieth-Century Poetry in English* (Oxford, Oxford University Press, 1994), 272.
2. *New York Times Book Review,* January 5, 1997.
3. *Washington Post,* November 27, 2005.

Dudley Felker Randall: Urban Trailblazer

1. Melba Joyce Boyd, ed., *Roses and Revolutions: The Selected Writings of Dudley Randall* (Detroit: Wayne State University Press, 2009), 4, 23.
2. Julius Thompson, *Dudley Randall, Broadside Press, and the Black Arts Movement in Detroit, 1960–1995* (Jefferson, NC: McFarland & Co., 1999), 29.

William McKendree Carleton: Verse Virtuoso

1. *Tri-City Herald*, Pasco, Kennewick, Richland, Washington, October 24, 1976, p. 14.

Marguerite de Angeli: Children Don't Forget

1. Ruth Heimbuecher, "Author Keeps Sense of Wonder," *Pittsburgh Press,* November 16, 1963.

Theodore Huebner Roethke: The Purity of Despair

1. Louis L. Martz, "A Greenhouse Eden," in *Theodore Roethke: Essays on the Poetry*, ed. Arnold Stein (Seattle: University of Washington Press, 1965).
2. John D. Boyd, "Texture and Form in Theodore Roethke's Greenhouse Poems," Modern Language Quarterly December 1971 32(4): 409–424.
3. Allan Seager, *The Glass House: The Life of Theodore Roethke* (Ann Arbor: University Michigan Press), 1991.

Maritta Wolff: Sudden Fame

1. Lilly March, "As Seen by Her," *Reading Eagle*, January 5, 1948, p. 6.

Liberty Hyde Bailey: A Bountiful Life

1. Pomology: the science and practice of fruit growing and variety development.
2. *New York Times*, November 23, 1901.
3. Diane M. Doberneck, paper prepared in conjunction with the launch of the Liberty Hyde Bailey Scholars Program, February 24, 1997.
4. *New York Times* obituary.
5. G.H.M. Lawrence, a colleague of Bailey at Cornell, in *Nature*, 1955.
6. Harry C. Boyte, codirector, Center for Democracy and Citizenship, Humphrey Institute of Public Affairs, University of Minnesota.
7. Harlan P. Banks, *Liberty Hyde Bailey, 1858–1954: A Biographical Memoir* (Washington, DC: National Academy of Sciences, 1994), 3.
8. Drawn from http://www.bsp.msu.edu/ShouldKnow/ProgramHistory/ TheLifeofLibertyHydeBailey/tabid/109/Default.aspx.

Ringgold Wilmer Lardner: Life Is More Than a Game

1. Quoted in M. K. Singleton, *H. L. Mencken and the American Mercury Adventure* (Durham: Duke University Press,1962).

Carl Sandburg: Sand Man

1. From Carl Sandburg, *Harvest Poems, 1910–1960* (San Diego: Harcourt, Brace, Jovanovich, 1960).

Charles Bruce Catton: America's Civil War Storyteller

1. Pages 370–71 of the 1956 edition.
2. *Banners at Shenandoah*, 130.
3. *Waiting for the Morning Train*, 49.
4. Ibid., 162–63.
5. Ibid., 235.

Sara Gwendolyn Frostic: Spirit Indomitable

1. For example, she made tiles that were installed in the structure.

John Donaldson Voelker: Great Character

1. From http://people.lis.illinois.edu/~unsworth/courses/bestsellers/search
   .cgi?title=anatomy+of+a+murder, accessed on January 30, 2012.
2. From Voelker interview, Michigan State University Sound Library.